Parrish Times

Parrish Times

My Life as a Racer

STEVE PARRISH

First published in Great Britain in 2018
by Weidenfeld & Nicolson

1 3 5 7 9 10 8 6 4 2

A CIP catalogue record for this book
is available from the British Library.

978 1 4746 07308

Typeset by Input Data Services Ltd, Somerset

Printed and bound by CPI Group (UK) Ltd, Croydon, CR0 4YY

Weidenfeld & Nicolson

The Orion Publishing Group Ltd
Carmelite House
50 Victoria Embankment
London EC4Y 0DZ

An Hachette UK Company
www.orionbooks.co.uk

*My two lovely children Frankie and Joe, and my wife Michelle –
and a massive thanks to Matt Roberts*

Acknowledgements

Sorry to Mum and Dad

Linda Davies, Ruth Wright, Michelle Parrish, Mr Caruthers (teacher), Mrs Wilson (head teacher), Mr Wainwright (head teacher)

Dawn and Jimmy Carter, John Brown (and thanks), Dave Morris, Jorge Lorenzo, Mike Trimby, Matt Roberts, Letchworth policeman, Hugh Chamberlain; and mechanics: Glen Bright, Dave Johnson, George Mansell, Martin Brookman, Adrian Gorst, Mick Jackson, Stuart and Simon Tonge

Alan Clarke, Dave Atkins, George Allan

Dave More, Charlie Cox, Chris Halmshaw, Geoff Sturgess, Belinda Rogerson, Rob McElnea, Terry Rymer, Carol McCutcheon, Dave Cunningham, Geoff Bennett, Richard Picking, Phil Corke, Jimmy and Zoë Sharples, Jack Burnicle, Barry Nutley, James Whitham, Mike Rowland, Carl Ward, Troy Corser

Judy, Shirley, Philip, school bus driver, Leigh Diffey, Ben Miller

Very sorry to Frankie and Joe . . .

. . . and all the people I've pissed off. 'Hard to dislike but worth the effort' has been said!

A note from Matt Roberts

After years of listening to Steve regaling people all over the world with these incredibly daft stories of his life, it has been a great pleasure to help him finally get them all down on paper, although as I fully expected the process hasn't been without its pitfalls.

After one weekend of working together at his house near Royston, I drove all the way back home to Huddersfield with the PEN15 number plate stuck to the back of my car and then left it parked outside the house for the whole of the following day before I realised. If I'd known about it I could have done the journey much more quickly!

I have also gone straight from his place to work at British Superbike events at Snetterton, Brands Hatch or Silverstone, where I've obliviously parked my car up in the paddock with various lewd stickers on the back. Of course, I was no stranger to these antics, having worked with Steve for seven years and travelled the world together as part of the BBC's MotoGP team, and having remained great friends ever since.

Steve's house is a monument to his irreverence, the first sign of which is the gentlemen's urinal hanging on the wall outside. Inside, an artificial parrot squawks 'Who's a pretty boy then?' when you turn off the bathroom light, which makes me jump every time, while the carpets are littered with fake dog turds and there is a life-size cut-out of Dean Martin standing in the shower. Among it all the Grand Prix trophies, framed newspaper clippings and faded photographs on the walls provide a fascinating tapestry of the hugely successful racing career that Steve is always eager to play down.

Our attempts to get all of that history and eccentricity onto the pages of this book were fuelled by the hot, home-made stews laid on by the long-suffering Michelle, which always made the long drives down to Hertfordshire worthwhile.

This spirit is captured perhaps most eloquently in the rare foreword that follows, written by a man who understood Steve better than anybody. Barry Sheene always encouraged his best friend to write this book and promised that he would pen the foreword. Just days before his death back in 2003, Barry told his wife Stephanie to grab a pen.

Matt Roberts

Foreword

I first met 'Stavros' in 1975, twenty-eight years ago, at Brands Hatch. 'Stavros' and I got on like a house on fire and seemed to see eye to eye with everything.

I invited him over to my place at Wisbech and haven't stopped laughing yet! I've never met anyone who can get themselves in and out of so much trouble.

If he could have set his bike up as well as his victims and have put as much effort into the bike racing as he did the intricate pranks he pulled on people he would certainly have been a World Champion.

As it was, he spent most of his time racing away from trouble. He was blindingly fast on four or six wheels, proven by five European truck racing titles.

Whatever he did, bikes, trucks, commentary, it would be fun for him and all around him.

Gas it wanker!

Barry Sheene

1

On thin ice

I am still not sure exactly how I found myself hurtling down a bobsleigh run upside down at over 60mph, with a drunken aristocrat giggling as he skidded along behind me, but I certainly know how it started. My great friendship with Barry Sheene had brought me into circles I would never normally have moved in, as we rubbed shoulders and other parts of our bodies with the great and the good of high society in swinging London. Since meeting Barry a couple of years earlier my life had suddenly become very interesting, and this was only the start.

It was the mid-1970s and Barry, of course, was a huge celebrity; a World Champion and the face of every marketing campaign from Texaco engine oils to Brut aftershave. And in his slipstream was me: his soon-to-be teammate and partner in crime, Stephen James Parrish, a farmer's son from Steeple Morden, Cambridgeshire. It wasn't a bad place to be, Barry's slipstream that is. I used to say it was like being in *Alice in Wonderland* and they weren't all called Alice!

Piers Weld-Forester was blue-blooded, the grandson of the 5th Marquis of Ormonde and twenty-fourth in line to the throne. He was so well connected to the royal family that he'd even dated Princess Anne. Piers had a really flash town house on Waterford Road in Chelsea, near the football ground, which must have been worth millions even then. We all had a key and we would go down for a week at a time, just hanging out together and having fun. The house had at least five or six bedrooms, one of which we called 'Room 7', which was Barry's room. Back then you could do whatever you wanted in London; drive at 90mph, park wherever you pleased and, of course, the nightlife was fantastic. We used to eat at a restaurant called 235 on the King's Road and we were regular patrons of Tramp, an exclusive members-only nightclub on Jermyn Street, which was very much the place to be at the time.

It is fair to say that Piers liked to live fast and despite his wealth and his Harrow education he was most intoxicated by the unique thrill of racing a motorcycle, which is how we first came to meet at Snetterton in 1976. His bike, a 750cc Yamaha, was quite worthy of the World Championship, but here he was, racing it in the Newmarket Club's local races. It was during that season that I would become British Champion for the first time myself and when Barry introduced us I was only too happy to help Piers out a bit with his racing. As a rider he would improve as time went on – he even started racing in some of the international events I was competing in – although the truth is that he wasn't very fast. We used to joke that Piers couldn't ride out of sight on a dark night but we all loved him. He was a wonderful character and, like everybody else, I just enjoyed being around him.

Even though on paper he was a millionaire, Piers was what I called a 'Trustafarian': asset rich, but never seemed to have any cash. All of the wealth he had was tied up, although he was able to get paid for attending the House of Lords: a hundred quid a day just for turning up and sitting at the back. So that's what he would do, usually passing the money straight on to an engine tuner called Roger Keen to pay for a new piston or something else for his race bike, which he kept in a garage underneath the house in Chelsea. He also had a van for his racing, a ten-year-old Ford Transit twin-wheeler, which he ran on red diesel. He would have the diesel delivered for the central heating in the flat, which somebody else must have been paying for, and then would siphon it off for his van. Piers seemed to know every scam in the book and over the next twelve months I would learn them all, soaking everything up like a sponge and loving every minute.

But in the winter of 1976 I didn't think much of it when he invited me off on an all-expenses-paid two-week skiing holiday to Igls, near Innsbruck. I'd never been skiing before. In fact, I'd hardly ever been out of the country before, so this sounded like an opportunity too good to miss. 'All you've got to do, Stavros,' he said, as we set off for Dover in the Transit, 'is pretend you can drive a bobsleigh when we get there.' I pictured a big group of lads mucking around on toboggans in some fancy ski resort and I rubbed my hands at the fun that was ahead.

When we got to the port Piers admitted that the ferry booking was actually for one person and a small car, so I took the hint to jump under a blanket in the back of the van while he negotiated our passage on board. As soon as we left the dock we headed straight to the lorry drivers' canteen where, wearing his Scania jacket for extra effect, Piers claimed he'd left his meal voucher in the truck and ordered himself a free serving of bacon and eggs. When he wanted to Piers could really talk the lorry drivers' lingo, despite his silver-spooned upbringing.

We made regular stops as we headed across Europe to buy red diesel from local farmers or else we simply siphoned it off from any tractors or diggers left unattended. We had local currency but I'm sure anything we did spend came out of my pocket. I was confused and amazed in equal measures by Piers and his manner which, it seemed, could help him get away with anything, but I was so green back then that I just went along with it.

Once into Germany we stopped off in Frankfurt, at a really swanky hotel. Of course, there were no mobile phones back then so, slipping back into his more natural persona of refined English gent, Piers politely told the receptionist that he would be checking in but first of all he had some urgent telephone calls to make, if they could kindly provide him with a line. With that old Harrovian accent of his, everything he said seemed plausible; they even agreed to arrange some lunch for the weary travellers. Sometime later, after a slap-up meal of schnitzel and potatoes, Piers ordered brandy, which was our cue to bolt out of the restaurant while the waiter's back was turned and make a sprint for the van. It was a scam I was to become familiar with for the remainder of our trip.

As we headed closer to Austria we made a slight detour to Switzerland. 'We just have to call in to St Moritz to pick up the bobsleigh from an old pal,' Piers explained. That seemed fair enough, but as we stepped into the outbuilding of this wealthy guy's winter getaway I felt that something wasn't quite right. There were chickens everywhere and this 'bobsleigh', which looked to me like the front end of an aeroplane, was all rusty and full of straw for the chickens. I asked Piers' pal why it had military badges on it and he explained that it had originally be-longed to the British Army. I didn't even want to know how it had ended up here. But Piers showed me around the bob, giving me some basic information like how the front runners turned but the rears were fixed, and with the help of Piers' pal and another chap the four of us lifted her into the back of the van.

There was one more stop to make before Igls, which was in Salzburg, where Piers disappeared into a building that turned out to be a brothel. Piers was eight years older than me and he'd spent quite a bit of time in the army, but talk about wide eyes and wet ears – I didn't even know what a brothel was, so I sat in the van for an hour and a half wondering what he was up to until he came back with a big smile on his face. He'd probably done a runner from there too.

As we headed on towards Igls I was finally furnished with some more key information about our trip, such as the fact that we'd actually be entering an event, along with around twenty or so other people. It still just sounded like a bit of fun. Finally, the next morning, we arrived at Igls, one of the few bobsleigh tracks in Europe that was, and still is, used all year round. That, of course, is why it was home to the British bobsleigh team and why we were now here: to take part in trials for the 1980 Winter Olympics.

Clearly this was a big surprise to me but back home the news was already out: 'Daredevil Duo Bob Off' read the headline in one of the nationals.

WITH the racing season over, Old Harrovian motorbike ace Piers Weld-Forester, 30, and British champion Steve Parrish, 22, are turning their daredevil attentions to a sport at the opposite end of the social scale.

Last night they left London by car en route for St Moritz to pick up a £2,000 bobsled in which they hope to secure a place in the British team for the World Championships in Cervinia, Italy, next year.

Piers, grandson of the 5th Marquis of Ormonde, and a rider for Yamaha, told me: 'I've done it once before, but Steve has never been in a bob. We'll decide who is going to drive after a couple of runs. I guess it will be the person least afraid.'

From St Moritz the intrepid duo will drive to Igls in Austria to take part in the British trials, which Prince Michael of Kent is supervising.

A place in the 1980 Winter Olympics is their eventual ambition.

Of course, as we now know, there are a few factual inaccuracies in the above report but I can't blame the journalist for any of that. However, Piers' royal connections and his talent for skiing had indeed brought him into contact with Prince Michael of Kent, who himself competed for Great Britain in the World Bobsleigh Championships in 1971. Now Prince Michael surely must have known that Piers was even less use on a bobsleigh than he was on a motorcycle, but somehow he'd allowed Piers to convince him that he had a competent driver lined up, an international motorcycle racer, no less, looking to turn his skill from the tarmac to the ice. The truth, of course, was that I had only clapped eyes on a bloody bobsleigh the day before, although compared to racing a two-stroke motorcycle at 170mph around the Isle of Man TT course it would surely be a walk in the park.

As I looked around the training camp at all these serious-looking athletes in their fancy tracksuits, buffing their shiny bobsleighs and sharpening the runners, I realised that out of the twenty or so British competitors there to race we were the only non-forces entry. There were teams from the army, navy, air force and marines, all of them probably having been told that Piers Weld-Forester was turning up with some shit-hot driver, and now here we were with all of them staring at us as we unloaded this rusty pile of junk from the back of an old Transit. I couldn't believe what I'd let myself in for but Piers assured me he knew the score, he'd done a bit of bobsleigh in the army and it was all going to be a complete doddle. He would be the brake-man and I would be the driver. For the first time since I'd been hanging out with Piers, I just wasn't convinced. 'What have I done?' I thought. What an embarrassment.

But at least it was free and that night, as I laid my head on a pillow for the first time in a few days, I thought that maybe something good was happening at last. The next morning we went for a look at the run we'd be going down. I took one peek over the side and almost shit myself. And that was only the first descent from the start! A bobsleigh is gravity-powered, so you only have to imagine how steep it has to be to get a bobsleigh and two passengers moving at speeds of up to 75mph. Beyond the start was no less daunting: a twisting, narrow, banked track with turns that can subject the crew to forces of up to 5g.

We were told that because of something to do with the temperature we could only practise first thing in the morning or late at night, so I could take the rest of the day off to worry about it. I would also need some special shoes, with hundreds of tiny spikes on the soles, so Piers took me to a local shop where I found myself parting with another forty quid just so I could push a rusty wreck down a concrete track covered in ice. It was too late to turn back now, so I reluctantly bought the shoes.

I kept looking at some of the other British teams and I could sense that they knew something was not right about Piers and me even being there. Their suspicions were confirmed when I arrived at the top of the track ready for our first practice run in full Texaco Heron Suzuki branded leathers and a full-face AGV motorcycle helmet. It was pretty clear that I didn't belong anywhere near these athletes in their Lycra suits and tight-fitting crash helmets, and worse still there was no sign of Piers. But we were scheduled to be the ninth crew away and I was told to get the bobsleigh on the ice in readiness.

Prince Michael called the first pairing up: 'Bob number one! Willis and Eversholt!' I was nervous and starting to get worried about Piers. Where the hell was he? To keep the runners from sticking to the ice you had to rock the bobsleigh back and forth, which was a tough enough task without my supposed teammate and brake-man missing and I quickly started to tire. I'd been rocking this rusty old piece of shit for about an hour when Prince Michael finally called for us: 'Bob number nine! Parrish and Forester!'

'I'm sorry, Your Highness, but my brake-man is running late,' I gasped. At this point one of the other British lads stepped forward and told me that Piers wouldn't go down the run until he was drunk and that he'd probably be in the bar. So Prince Michael sent for him and eventually he appeared, looking a little glassy-eyed and giddy but at least now seemingly up for the challenge.

'Ready, sir,' I nervously declared.

'Very well, Parrish. As you are and go.'

To start a bobsleigh you're supposed to rock it back and forth and then take a big run before plunging down the first descent. Not us. We crept it carefully to the edge and gingerly jumped in as it gathered momentum for the first turn, Piers giggling all the way. I'd worked out that the idea was to get as high as possible on the bends to gather speed for the straights and in no time we were flying along at around 60mph, although even for a motorcycle racer accustomed to doing well over double that speed it felt much faster. The steering system, which is basically two metal rings on a pulley system that operate the runners, is really sensitive, so at that speed it's very easy to turn yourself upside down. Inevitably, by the third corner, that is exactly what I did.

In this situation, we had been briefed, the procedure was for the brake-man to jump out of the back of the bobsleigh and drag the driver out as soon as possible. The main reason for this was to protect the ice from damage, although obviously it's a safety issue too. You can then either turn the bobsleigh over and continue your run or simply let it go on its own, as the bobs are designed to right themselves and cruise to the finish. But, of course, Piers was rendered completely powerless by the booze and now was in fits of laughter, leaving me trapped in the front of the bob as we scraped and scratched our way down the remainder of the track.

We crossed the line at 62mph, which I think must be a record for an upside-down bob, but the ice behind us was completely wrecked and we got the most incredible bollocking. But the truth is I was relieved; we were in one piece, our cover was surely blown and now maybe we could get out of there and go skiing.

However, we were given one more chance and at 5 a.m. the next morning Prince Michael came into our room to wake us. He was greeted with the strange sight of me lying in bed, fast asleep, with my crash helmet on to block out the noise of Piers' snoring. Once again, it must have occurred to the Prince what complete twats we were. But once again he guided us to the top of the track, asking me where exactly I had competed before. I recited some of the names of bobsleigh tracks that Piers had drilled into me during our journey to Igls. Prince Michael told me that two of our rival competitors had broken their arms the day before, so I grabbed hold of Piers, still pissed from the night before, and told him we needed to give it a proper go this time.

Again we edged gingerly over the precipice but we were soon skimming along the ice and this time I remained completely focused on keeping us upright. By the fifth corner we were upside down again, and we were still upside down at turns six, seven, eight, nine . . . all the way to the finish. In fact, turn five was as far as I ever got the right way up in my bobsleigh career because thankfully, this time, we were asked to leave. Prince Michael told us we weren't taking it seriously enough, that we looked ridiculous in our motorcycle leathers and helmets and with our drinking and carrying on we weren't fit to represent

Great Britain in the manner expected. It was hard to argue with him really.

So we happily left the bobsleigh behind and jumped back into the old Transit, with our travel allowance in Piers' pocket, and made our way to the Stubai Glacier, where we finally got that skiing holiday. Of course, I again made myself look like a complete prat by turning up on the slopes in an anorak and jeans and then wiping out an entire queue of around thirty people waiting for the chair lift. I really had no clue about what I was doing back then, and many people would tell you that I still don't, but my education had just begun.

Unfortunately, there would be precious few further adventures with Piers. The following autumn, during a race meeting at Brands Hatch, he slid off his prized Yamaha TZ750 on the exit of Clearways, the last corner on the track, and went straight into the barriers. I was at the event, although I was racing in a different class, so I could see the crash from the pits and I could see it was bad. The ambulance took him off to Queen Mary's and we never saw him again. Piers' death shocked us all, and it was front page news in the national papers.

The *Daily Mirror* – Monday, 31 October 1977

Tragedy of the fearless playboy
by George Fallows

PLAYBOY racer Piers Weld-Forester, a former boyfriend of Princess Anne, was killed yesterday in a high-speed motorcycle crash.

Thirty-one-year-old Piers tumbled from his bike during the opening race of an international meeting at Brands Hatch.

He slid across the track, crashed into a protective barrier and died later from multiple injuries in Queen Mary's Hospital, Sidcup, Kent.

Handsome Piers, grandson of the Marquis of Ormonde, was the darling of the racing circuits.

He was high society's Action Man, fast with machines . . . and the ladies.

Piers first met Princess Anne in 1971 at the home of the Earl of Lichfield, another aristocratic bike buff.

Over the following months he often took her out to dinner. And once escorted her to the theatre to see the musical Godspell.

He told friends: 'She's never been on my pillion. I think she prefers horses.'

But he still thought the Princess was pretty good on two wheels when she rode Lord Lichfield's motorbike.

'She's one of the quickest people I've seen,' he said.

But there were many other women in Piers' life – all of them beautiful.

They were clearly turned on by his fearless sense of adventure.

He got his kicks from free-fall parachuting, bobsleighing, racing cars and fatally fast motorbikes.

But his one attempt at settling down with the woman he loved ended in tragedy.

After only nine months of marriage his lovely bride, model Georgina Youens, was among the 345 victims of the 1974 Paris air crash.

Piers, who ran a haulage firm and wine importing business, deadened his grief the only way he knew how – with fast machines.

He put his heart into motorbike racing and became a firm favourite with everyone from mechanics to sponsors.

On meetings abroad he became the British riders' shop steward because of his knowledge of foreign languages.

It was on one of those meetings, in France just a year ago,

15

that devil-may-care Piers got a warning of the fate that was to befall him.

He came off a bike under almost identical conditions to yesterday's fatal crash.

As he lay on the stretcher, he heard one of the first aid team say they thought he was dead.

Piers, very much alive, sat up and laughed.

Undaunted, fearless, Piers also nearly killed himself in a crash in Yugoslavia during the Paris to Persia motorcycle rally.

Even that didn't stop his lust for speed.

Last year he and a friend bought a £2,000 bobsleigh and hoped to win a place at the 1980 Winter Olympics.

When Piers crashed yesterday, the eight-lap race was immediately stopped.

A mark of respect for a man who loved the fast life.

Any hopes Piers might have had of competing in the US, of course, had been left a long way behind at Igls, but I'll always cherish the memory of our pathetic attempt! A couple of years later I was back in more familiar territory, sitting on the start line at the Formula 1 motorcycle TT on the Isle of Man. Even back then the TT was one of the most dangerous events in the world and with two hours of racing around that infamously perilous 37.73-mile road circuit ahead, the last thing you want is to talk to anybody. As usual, I was nervous as hell and desperately keen to get the race started but as I looked up I saw a group of dignitaries walking towards me. Leading the party was Prince Michael of Kent, now the honorary President of the Auto-Cycle Union. As he approached he bent down slowly and looked straight into my visor. 'Ah, Parrish,' he said. 'I do hope you're better at this than you were at bobsleigh!'

2

Baby driver

My nickname, 'Stavros', was given to me by Barry Sheene when he saw a picture of me as a child. With my chubby frame and tight curls, he reckoned I looked like George Savalas's character from the TV show *Kojak*. To be fair it was a pretty accurate lookalike: I was a fat little bastard and a troublemaker too.

I was born at Church Farm in the village of Steeple Morden in Cambridgeshire in 1953. The farmhouse was large, rambling and draughty with very creaky stairs and rattling windows. It had been bought by my grandfather, Bert Parrish, shortly before he died and left a mountain of debt behind. Bert had been a castrator and cattle dealer, so I reckon that is where my natural talent for talking bollocks and bullshit came from. After Bert died the farm was sold to a mortgage company, but my father Graham continued to work it, growing Brussels sprouts, sugar beet and cereal crops, until eventually he raised enough money to buy it back in 1947, six years before I was born there.

I was the youngest of a family of four; my sisters Shirley and Judy came first, then my brother Phil and then, seven years later, me. It doesn't take a great mathematician to work out that I was probably a mistake and I never really had a close relationship with any of my siblings, who were all packed off to boarding school in Bedfordshire long before I can remember. I guess by the time I came along my father had two lovely daughters and a son who helped him about the farm, whereas I was a little pain in the arse that he could have done without. I don't remember there being much love there; nobody ever kissed or cuddled in my family. I was never tucked up in bed, just sent off to my room to get on with it myself.

Don't worry, this isn't the classic 'difficult childhood' chapter. In fact, I was very happy growing up on that bustling farm, free to roam the countryside that I love and getting into mischief. We had a couple of milking cows so there was always a large jug of fresh cream on the breakfast table and my mother, Bay, would make her own butter. But when looking after number one actually became my profession, as a motorcycle racer in my early twenties, I would have loved to have taken one of my trophies home to my dad. 'You were wrong about me,' I would have said. 'I am not as stupid as you thought.' But unfortunately I never got that chance. My father died of leukaemia when I was 12 years old. By that time, he had already spent a year in and out of hospital and I hadn't been allowed to visit, so I didn't know him very well at all.

When my father died I was sent away to my best friend Geoff Sturgess's family and I stayed with them for a couple of weeks until they had buried father and the whole thing had blown over. Looking back it seems quite a strange thing to have happened, and I'm sure it upset me at the time, but I can't say I remember missing my father. What I do remember is that he kept a stick above the mantelpiece in the dining room and if I was bad he was under strict instructions from my mother to give me a thrashing. I threw that stick on the fire the moment I came back from the Sturgesses' and I have been a law unto myself ever since.

My mother really was a tough old lady after Pops popped

off but eventually I think I did drive her mad. In later life she developed Alzheimer's but probably thought she'd had early onset for many years prior to that, when I would swap the hard-boiled eggs she had marked and put in the fridge for raw ones. During her latter years mother continued to live, with the help of a nurse, in the family home, which meant I was often in charge of making sure she didn't wander off. Early one morning I was on duty when she managed to slip out and find her way to the village garage, owned by the Prothero family, where she climbed into a car that was sitting on the hydraulic service ramp. A mechanic came into work shortly after and, completely oblivious to her presence, pressed the lift button to commence a full service and brake lines. I was looking for her all day while she sat in that car until around 5 p.m., when the mechanic finally lowered the ramp back down and had the living shit scared out of him by my poor mother!

Finally mum passed away in 1988 and it was decided that we would spread her ashes in Norfolk, as per her instructions. I couldn't go so it was my brother who drew the short straw to take the urn and meet my sister, who lives there. What they didn't know was that I got hold of the urn before them, undid the wax, took the lid off and dropped two glass eyes in there. For extra surprise effect I took my daughter Frankie's old jack-in-the-box to pieces and carefully jammed that in there too. On the evening before they were planning to spread mum's ashes at a local beauty spot, they were at my sister's house when curiosity got the better of them and they decided to have a peek in the urn. They had hardly touched the seal when the lid flew off and the jack flew out. My sister dropped the lot and the glass eyes came bouncing out from the ashes and rolled across the kitchen floor!

It turned out that my eldest sister Shirley did have a sense of humour after all, because when I phoned up later – concerned that I had not heard anything and might have finally gone too far – she told me there'd been a change of plan and they had left the ashes for the vicar to distribute. 'Bloody hell, I've really gone too far this time!' I thought, and I was just getting in the car in a genuine panic to fly down to the vicarage and prevent a catastrophe when I got a message from Phil to say they were having me on!

But for many years mother had somehow kept the farm going by herself and I had free run of the place because she was so busy. If I played hooky from school nobody cared and mum rarely found out anyway because I would change the school reports and Tippex over my attendance rate. The one time this tactic failed to help me was on the day I bunked off to go to the Newmarket horse races and mum saw me on the television! There was nothing she could really do to reprimand me though and since there was no discipline at home I had nothing to worry about at school either.

By then I had already been expelled once, from the village primary school, while my father was still alive. Admittedly I probably deserved it because I wrote a message on the school wall for the attention of the headmistress. It simply read: 'Mrs Wilson is a fat old cow.' I had spelt it correctly and everything but still for some reason they weren't impressed. It just happened to be a Friday evening, so my parents were having a dinner party when a policeman came and knocked on the door. Me and Geoff – whom I'd roped into helping me – my parents and their dinner guests in all their evening finery had to go around to the school and scrub it off. My sister Shirley wasn't impressed either, because Mrs Wilson used to give her lifts to Ashwell station sometimes, and that put a stop to it.

Church Farm was around five hundred acres of mainly arable land, which incorporated Steeple Morden airfield, a supplementary base to RAF Bassingbourn that was home to Wellington bombers during the war. One of the ways in which my father had generated the capital to buy the land back from the bank had been to break up the concrete runways and sell the rubble to the contractors building the M1. Originally these runways would have been up to a hundred metres wide but when they broke them up they reduced them to normal road width, so that you could still drive around them as well as the perimeter tracks and other roads to get in and around the farm. At least, that was what they were intended for. But now that I was in charge, this sprawling web of concrete track was to become my own personal racetrack.

I developed a love of anything with an engine from a very young age. It all started with a ride-on mower that I would spend hours taking apart, rebuilding and then driving around. Then my brother Phil fuelled my interest, driving Geoff and me around the airfield in cars he bought for a few quid and then trashed. One particular favourite was to set a car off with the accelerator pedal tied down in the direction of an old bomb shelter, willing it to fly over the shelter! It never did. And before long I was driving the cars myself, and crashing them too.

The airfields were also used by an engineering company from nearby Letchworth, called Borg Warner, to test gearboxes and I remember my father once telling me not to go up as there was a Jaguar XK150 being driven about. Of course, I bombed up anyway in my mother's Renault Dauphine, barely able to see over the steering wheel, and this poor test driver careered into the next field, probably thinking there was a driverless car coming straight for him. Shortly after my father died I pinched the keys to his Humber Super Snipe and took Geoff on a drive down to Letchworth. We put cushions on the seat, trilby hats on our heads and drove around town, just because we could.

Anything mechanical floated my boat – the smell, the noise

and how it all worked just fascinated me – and I started to develop an obsession with speed. It's hard to say where that came from because nobody in my family had it. Even my son prefers a football to an engine, which I think is quite weird, but for me there was only one thing I was interested in doing and that was driving fast. I started saving whatever little money I could earn from washing people's cars and began buying my own, picking up scrap vehicles for five or ten quid and then working out how to get them going again up on the airfield. Sometimes my mates would chip in, in exchange for free rides, and occasionally I got little donations from family members like my brother Phil or my uncle Freddie Tyrell, who on occasion even found and bought old cars for me.

Motorcycles were commonplace back then because in the years after the Second World War there had been so many people using them as an affordable means of daily transport. I remember I picked up a 500cc Matchless, a Velocette, a BSA 250, a Triumph scooter . . . to be honest, really, it didn't matter what kind of bike it was or even what kind of vehicle; it could be a bike, a car or a pickup truck – if it had wheels and an engine that I reckoned I could get going, I bought it. One of my pals was a boy called Paul Prothero, whose father owned the petrol station and garage where my poor mother would many years later get stuck in that bloody car. So Paul was in charge of supplying the fuel. He'd come up with two gallons, we'd tip it into whatever vehicle we'd got our hands on and drive around until it ran out. If I couldn't get something moving I would just pinch a tractor from the farm and tear around in that.

I was carefree, fearless of the consequences and an attention seeker, a show-off. People would say 'Fucking hell, that boy Parrish can drive!' and of course, since I wasn't academic and wasn't being shown much affection at home, I courted that attention. Many of my mates' parents didn't even have cars, yet they could come and jump in the passenger seat with me and be going sideways round a corner in an Austin 16 with the tyres smoking until they fell off. I loved the speed, I loved scaring myself and I loved getting away with it. Above all, though, I loved entertaining others.

Often I'd take a tractor down to Bassingbourn Youth Club and charge the other kids a bob or two to ride up and down in the front-loader bucket. My mum was too busy to know what I was up to, although all the farm workers used to hate me, as you can imagine. We had a couple of guys there driving the tractors and suchlike and they'd often jump in to find them with a flat tyre or out of diesel because I'd run them dry. No wonder they hated me so much, I really can't blame them. On one occasion my brother had let a friend of his store a Chevrolet Corvette Stingray at the farm so I nicked it and drove down to the youth club in that. I wasn't even old enough to drive but there I was, cruising down to the youth club in this beautiful American sports car.

Geoff was my next-door neighbour and partner in crime until we were in our early teens, when his parents finally decided to move away because I was such a bad influence. Mr and Mrs Sturgess were both academics and they envisioned a similar future for their son, so I guess him being dragged around a field on a toboggan towed by a car driven by a 10-year-old hooligan wasn't quite what they had in mind. Geoff was always so game though, and when I started riding motorcycles he would jump on the back with me as I charged down the old runways at speed, seeing if we could get 80mph out of an old 500cc Matchless I had picked up. I tried to teach him how to ride on a BSA 250, but he got confused about which way to twist the throttle and went faster and faster until he hit a rabbit warren.

We would spend hours together playing in the straw stacks, exploring the outhouses and eating 'docky' from Oxo tins with the workers on their lunch break. Being a working farm, we had a shotgun in the cupboard, which my mother never locked, so we would just grab some cartridges and go out shooting anything we could; wildlife, glass bottles, rusty old cars – it didn't matter to us. We would regularly break into the local garage to steal cigarettes and sweets, which formed my staple diet, so it's no wonder I was such a fat little bastard. The other kids at school called me Jumbo and even to this day I have a cartoon of an elephant on my helmet. When the summer evenings started to get dark we would ride past the village bobby Constable Fuller's house with no lights on our bicycles and see how far we could get before he caught us.

This was all great entertainment to us but for Mrs Sturgess I think the final straw came when she looked out of her kitchen window to see Geoff and me jumping up and down on the asbestos roof of an outbuilding. Geoff went straight through, falling twenty feet to the concrete floor below. I honestly thought he had finally bought it and I ran off into the field shouting: 'Geoffrey's dead! Geoffrey's dead!'

Eventually the Sturgesses put their house up for sale and I was so upset when I saw the sign outside that I stole the washing from their line and buried it in the garden. My best friend, the only real bit of company I had on that farm, was being taken away and I was devastated, although I suppose my actions merely confirmed to the Sturgesses that they were making the right decision. Geoff went on to become a successful solicitor, so it's hard to argue with their choice!

After my first expulsion I got sent to a private school in Cambridge called The Shrubbery. I don't know whether my mother thought I would get into less trouble there or if it was a case of 'out of sight, out of mind', but it didn't work because

I was constantly bunking off to ride my motorbike across the local fields up to the village college to see my friends. The bobbies caught hold of me once and took the bike off me, so my mum had to pick me up. I wasn't doing anybody any harm but I was developing a reputation for being the bad lad of the neighbourhood. I loved the thrill of the chase and the adrenaline rush of doing something I wasn't supposed to do.

On the days I did attend The Shrubbery I would have to take a tremendously tedious bus ride, which would take about an hour, so clearly not being the most patient of children I came up with ways to entertain myself, and others. One of my favourite moves was to tie crop scarers, which were big exploding bangers on a slow-burning fuse that farmers used to frighten off birds, to the back of the bus. Every ten minutes or so there'd be a tremendous 'BANG!' causing the confused driver to stop and check over the vehicle. I would just be cooped up on the bus sniggering to myself, already chalking off the minutes that I was saving myself from being sat in lessons! Amazingly I never got caught for that one but it was my creativity with my engineering skills that eventually brought a premature end to my education.

Quite simply, I started to treat my teachers like the morons they thought I was. Why did I need to know algebra when I could put a set of points in a car and go fast around a field? I never liked geography much and had a particular dislike for the teacher of that subject, Mr Caruthers. So I decided to loosen the wheel nuts on his Triumph Herald, put the hub-caps on, and watched with great delight as he drove out of the school yard before all four wheels dropped off.

There was no denying that one, so I was promptly expelled from The Shrubbery and sent off to do an apprenticeship, which was the way the education system dealt with misunderstood children at the time. It suited me though, because I truly hated school and I have never been burdened with knowledge as a result. I remember the headmaster Mr Wainwright telling me I was a moron and I would never achieve anything in my life. But I started with nothing and I've still got most of it left, so who was right?

I was sent to join a local agricultural engineering company called Weatherheads of Royston, which was perfect. Finally I had a purpose in life. I was getting up of a morning to go to work, where from the moment I arrived I was mending tractors and other farming equipment, developing a skill set that had been hidden by my supposed stupidity, and meeting mates of the same age with the same interests. Then there were older blokes who'd been there for years that I could look up to; they knew a lot, they could teach me things and they wouldn't think twice about smacking me around the earhole if I stepped out of line. As soon as I found something I liked doing I became more active, more healthy and I lost all that baby fat that many years later would earn me my nickname from Barry.

Back then an apprenticeship was supposed to last for five years; four days at work and a day's release at college. But I was so handy with a spanner that after a year at Weatherheads they started sending me off to farms to do callout jobs on my own, while still paying me apprentice wages. After a couple of years there I got accused of bodging a job, which was absolute rubbish, so I walked out and picked up my apprenticeship with another local company called Collins Brothers – who did exactly the same thing, only instead of fixing Massey Ferguson tractors they fixed Leylands – on better wages. I loved it there, although I'm not sure they felt the same way about me – especially when I wired the clocking-in machine up to the spark plug testing machine. If you were two minutes late you would get docked an hour, so every morning at eight all of the lads were pushing and shoving each other out of the way to get to the machine and about four of them got a massive electric shock for their troubles! I got thrown into the lake when they found out it was me, but it was well worth the soaking.

The extra cash I was now earning was allowing me to pursue my interest in motorbikes, and I counted down the days to when I could finally get my licence and ride them on the roads. I took my test in Stevenage on my sixteenth birthday on a Yamaha YDS3 250cc, the maximum I was allowed to ride at that time with a provisional licence, which I bought from Hallens of Cambridge for £225. The bike test was unbelievably simple back then: the instructor just stood on the pavement and told you to set off down the road, go right, right and right again and come back around the block, then on the second lap he'd hold his hand out for you to make an emergency stop. That was it. I had my licence!

Three days later I went down to Hallens and swapped the Yamaha, which was constantly seizing, for a 650cc BSA A10, which seemed so fast to me at the time. Paul Prothero had a relatively new BSA Lightning, which for some stupid reason he lent to me. Of course, I wrung its neck, maximum revs in every gear until it finally blew a huge hole in the crank case. I had to wheel it round to his house with the con rod poking out of the side and I couldn't have felt worse about it if I'd shagged his girlfriend. Personally, I'd prefer to let my best mate shag my girlfriend than bring my bike back looking like that. I ended up buying the bike off him and finding the parts to repair the blown engine.

I rode a motorcycle to work every day that I had one running and each day I would pass a house with a bloke out the front working on his own motorcycle. I was intrigued by this fellow so one day I stopped by to talk to him about his bike. The man's name was Roger Brown and he turned out to be the very first motorcycle racer I had ever met. Roger was a tall, good-looking guy but he was quiet and humble, more bothered about the mechanics of racing motorcycles than the glamour or the lifestyle. To me, the very idea that you could race motorcycles around a circuit was completely new. There was no racing on television back then and I didn't get *Motor Cycle News* or anything like that. I was absolutely intrigued and straight away I offered to give Roger a hand.

Roger let me help him clean the wheels of his race bikes, fetch the fuel, things like that, and he soon became the first role model I had ever had; I hung on his every word. He would go off racing on a weekend and on Monday morning I would be straight down to look at the trophies he had won and examine any photographs he had of the races, pestering him to take me along to the next meeting. Eventually Roger agreed and I went to my first ever race at Snetterton in 1972. From the moment I walked in through the gates I was hooked on that intoxicating mix of the atmosphere, the smell and the sounds of the paddock. Up to that point I didn't have much direction in my life but instantly I knew that now I did. My world would never be the same again.

3

Pourus Racing

Speed, engines, beer and danger. The motorcycle racing paddock really was utopia for me and whenever Roger wasn't competing at the races I would go along myself. Driving my Singer Gazelle, I'd round up a bunch of mates who were easily led from the Coach and Horses pub in Harston near Cambridge and head off for Brands Hatch or Snetterton, where they would all have to squeeze into the boot so that we only paid for one ticket. I had no idea if I would or could be fast enough to race myself but all the lads were convinced that I was, so together we built a bike out of old parts that we'd sourced from ads in *Exchange and Mart* and made a plan to enter an upcoming club race at Brands.

The bike was a Triton Hybrid; a pre-unit 1968 500cc Triumph Tiger 100 engine that I had bought for £22, housed in a Norton Featherbed frame. I was so pleased with myself. It was the ultimate Rocker's machine: swept-back pipes, alloy tank, oil pissing out of the primary chain case and brakes that could barely stop a wheelbarrow. But boy did it look good, and on the rare occasions that I got it running on both cylinders, it sounded the bollocks too.

One of the lads from the pub was John Elbourne, an archetypal leather-clad Rocker with long hair who also fancied a go at racing, so we clubbed together to buy an old Commer box van from a greengrocer. It was completely knackered. It used gallons of oil and had a fuel pump problem, so we stood a jerrycan on top of the engine compartment between the two front seats of the van, with a gravity feed pipe down to the carburettor.

In the same way that other pubs have a darts or cricket team, the Coach and Horses now had a motorcycle racing team and each one of the lads had a role. Bill Beadle, a tall, fair-haired lad who could make and machine anything we needed, became our engineer and he spent half the time at the firm where he worked making things for my bike. Bernie Abs was a panel beater and sprayer by trade so he took care of the bodywork, little Bernie Dillon was our unassuming, sensible electrician, Rob Henry was a suave operator with a Lotus Cortina so he looked after PR duties, writing letters about me to magazines and the local newspaper, Patsy Cook was the comedian of the bunch (possibly even funnier than me) so he provided the entertainment and John and I were the riders. We called ourselves 'Pourus Racing' because the van was leaking so much oil and we were 'poor as piss'.

Since we weren't quite sure how many times the old shed would break down on the way to our first race, we loaded the bikes up and left before the sun came up to head to Brands Hatch. The trip would take two hours with a tail wind and no malfunctions, which remarkably was exactly what happened, so we rolled into Brands at around five in the morning for a scrutineering appointment at eight.

Needless to say, we were full of trepidation. Frankly, we were shitting ourselves at the thought of actually getting out on that beautiful but terrifying ribbon of tarmac, so we looked to park the van as close to the lavatories as possible. As we cruised around the paddock looking for a good spot, I inadvertently hooked up the guy rope of some poor sod's tent on the bumper of the van and dragged the whole lot – camping stove, kettle, sleeping incumbents and all – about thirty yards to the toilet block. I only realised it had happened when I opened the door to be greeted by the strange sight of four people sitting up in their sleeping bags shouting abuse at me. Typical of me, I did a runner to the toilets and left John to sort the mess out, which he proved quite adept at, and half an hour later we were all sitting around their re-erected tent enjoying a nice cup of tea.

I don't think it was Norton's idea when they came up with the 'Featherbed' name but the bike certainly handled like a bed and it managed just eight laps in practice before one of the footrests fell off and the rev counter bracket snapped. Those old Triton engines notoriously leaked like a baby with diarrhoea, as anybody who has ever owned one will know, so to top it all my boots were covered in oil. However, with a scheduled distance of eight laps the bike would just about make it to the flag and after a race-long battle with a guy on a 500cc single I too went down to one cylinder on the final lap and dropped all the way back to last place. It was incredible that I made the finish at all really, because when I looked down at the bike most of the barrel nuts had come off and the alloy cylinders were going up and down with the pistons. It was an ugly sight.

John's race didn't go much better either. He had a really good job at a local printing factory, so he had been able to afford a proper bike, a Westlake Triumph in a Metisse frame, which he fell off that day and just about every other time he rode it. Given that we started racing at the same time, and especially with him being ten years older and on far better equipment than me, John was a real benchmark for me to measure my progress against over the coming weeks and months. Whenever he did stay on and my Triton held together I would beat him quite easily, so even though I soon started to get fed up of being covered in oil our results gave me the confidence to think that this racing lark might be an activity worth pursuing.

The other person I have to thank for not jacking the whole job in at that early stage was another member of our intrepid pub team, John Wright, a gangly grafter with an amazing mullet and an equally impressive ability to make money, who is known to this day as 'Frog', I've no idea why. Frog had a great little business buying, selling and repairing lawnmowers and he was always the wealthiest of the bunch: thankfully, he decided to spend some of it on me. I suppose, like many philanthropists with a passion for racing, he didn't fancy trying it himself but he was dead keen to get involved in some capacity. I guess he saw a little potential in me and he was enjoying what we were doing, so he managed to find a properly built Triton with a Triumph Bonneville engine, which he bought and very kindly loaned to me. The bike was a belter and, hey presto, I started winning club races on it! I still see Frog nowadays and I never forget the debt of gratitude I owe him.

The fact that we had gone from the back of the races to the front overnight got the whole team excited. Bill Beadle would come around to my place in the morning after spending all night making more lightweight parts and Bernie Dillon came up with a better ignition. I'd spend Friday night putting the bike together in a workshop I had set up at the farm and then first thing on Saturday morning we'd be round to pick everybody up in the van and off we went to Snetterton or Brands Hatch; and sometimes up to Cadwell Park if we had enough money between us for the fuel. None of us even considered at that point that one of us was going to make a living out of racing; it hadn't even entered our heads. Racing was just a giggle, a way of having fun at weekends and passing the time before we went to the pub in the evening. If we came home with a trophy then the beer tasted even sweeter as we hatched our plan for the following weekend.

What I did know was that I wasn't going to be completing my apprenticeship at Collins Brothers. As well as working on my own bike, I was using the workshop at the farm to run my own little repair business, which I called Kerbside Motors, fixing anything from tractors to trucks, cars, scooters and mopeds, and I quickly developed a head for numbers. I remember a lady came in to have her Citroën serviced, which I did a thorough job of, even removing the spare tyre to examine it for any defects. When she came back to collect her car I forgot to put the spare tyre back and had every intention of returning it to her but got waylaid, like you do. The tyre remained in the back of the workshop for months before, as luck would have it, she returned. 'Can you help, Steve?' she asked. 'Only, I've got a flat tyre and somebody has stolen my spare. You wouldn't happen to have a tyre that fits my car would you?' After scrambling about for a few minutes I produced a tyre that was the perfect fit and it is fair to say that we were both happy with the outcome! It didn't take me long to figure I could make money in other ways. I would buy a banger like an old Triumph Herald for ten quid, weld it up and get it through its MOT, respray it, clock it, sell it on for double the money and then blow the lot on racing!

So with Pourus Racing now propped up by a teenaged entrepreneur, the next step was to invest in a better motorcycle. I had become friendly with a very handy club racer called Roger Keen, who lived close to me. Roger was probably the best engine builder I had ever met but he was so annoying because he never had anything ready when he said it would be. Any job with Roger would take days or even weeks, rather than hours, and I reckon I probably spent a year of my life waiting for a crankshaft to emerge from his workshop.

He was slow in the workshop but fast on the track and we enjoyed nothing more than finishing the weekend with one last race in our vans on the way home. Proper tie-downs had yet to be invented so with the bikes held up by nothing but washing line rope and us driving like a pair of complete lunatics, I am pretty sure that during the 1972 season we did more damage to our race bikes in the back of the vans than we ever did to them on the track.

Roger had a Yamaha TD2B250 in the yellow and black Yamaha USA colours that would later be made famous by rising American superstar Kenny Roberts. Whether it was that iconic livery or the fact that he was winning lots of races on it, I fell in love with that bike instantly and I was desperate to have it myself. In the October of 1972, after much badgering, Roger finally agreed to sell it to me and I put down a deposit of £250, which I borrowed from my mum. I took delivery of the bike in the middle of the following March, the day before my first race of the 1973 season.

I had a great year on that little Yamaha, winning loads of club races and championships. The boys from the pub would still come with me and make some odds and ends for the bike, but the burgeoning success of our endeavours would inevitably mean that the days of Pourus Racing were numbered. The end effectively came a year or so later at Snetterton in 1974, when I was sitting working on the bike. I was approached by a kind-looking man who introduced himself as Harold Coppock, a benevolent former chicken farmer who had sold his business for a lot of money and now ran his own race team called the 'Coppock Superchicks'.

Harold was such a generous, salt-of-the-earth man who was like a grandfather to a whole bunch of riders in the paddock and he said he'd been keeping an eye on me all season. He had been impressed with what I was doing on the TD2B250, which was a good bike but an old model, and he said he felt that I could do even better on more up-to-date machinery, which he was willing to lend me if I rode for him. I agreed to drive down to his beautiful house in Carterton, Oxfordshire, where he showed me into a huge workshop with loads of Yamahas in it. Harold explained that he already sponsored a Welsh guy called Wayne Dinham and wanted a second rider. He would pay the entry fees and even loaned me a signwritten van with the team name on the side, which actually had an MOT and didn't need a jerrycan of fuel on the front seat. I had arrived!

I would still have to cover the cost of fuel, tyres and repairs, so any money I earned from my business or prize money at the race meetings would all go straight back into all of that. But I could hardly believe my luck as I loaded a TZ250 and a TZ350 into my van and took them back up to my workshop. I was still very much an amateur but the whole thing was getting more serious. I would be racing most weekends at places like Croft, Scarborough and other circuits all over the country, and the lads just weren't able to muck in as much as they used to.

Harold was like a fairy godfather to me. He would turn up one week with a new seat or a new set of pistons and then go off and sit with his wife in their big Mercedes, watching the races over a flask of coffee and a hamper of sandwiches. Later on during that first season, he even picked up a third rider called Mick Patrick and over the next couple of seasons we had a fair amount of success between us.

The standout meeting for me during that time was a club event at Brands Hatch in 1974 called 'Stars of Tomorrow'. It was designed to unearth new young motorcycle talent and my hero would be there as one of the judges. Barry Sheene was already an international superstar; a playboy racer who was not just one of the most famous faces in British sport at the time but also a symbol of popular culture during the seventies. He was a good-looking, cheeky Cockney with a quick wit, an eye for the ladies and a taste for champagne, so his off-track antics alongside other famous faces of the day, as well as the aristocracy, in the exclusive nightclubs of swinging West London made him a headline writer's dream. It is hard to think of a modern-day equivalent of Barry Sheene because they truly 'don't make 'em like that any more', but he was every bit as much a celebrity and a cultural icon as David Beckham is now.

Alongside the likes of George Best and James Hunt, Barry was one of the first athletes ever to transcend his sport and he was on the front and back pages of every tabloid newspaper, but to me there were only two publications that mattered: *Motor Cycle News* and *Motor Cycle Weekly*, which I would buy and devour with great enthusiasm every week, reading about Barry's exotic exploits in the 500cc World Championship and pulling out the posters of him to pin on my wall.

I had a stonking meeting at Brands, winning the 250cc race, the 350cc race and one of the open races, all on my little TZ250. There was somebody else there who won the 750cc race but I won three out of the four events and even broke the club lap record. Somehow, however, when it went down to the judges I was awarded second place.

At the end of the meeting Barry came up to me and said: 'Fuck knows what that other lot were looking at but I voted for you.' To be honest, I think he had an eye on my girlfriend Linda, even though he was with his girlfriend Leslie at the time, but we got chatting and with Barry living in Wisbech and me just down the road from Royston we figured out we'd be going the same way home, so we arranged to stop for a bite to eat on the way. It's hard to believe now but in 1974 there was no M25 or anything like that, so the quickest way from Brands Hatch back to Cambridgeshire was to go into

London, through the Blackwall Tunnel and back out again. So we stopped somewhere south of the river for dinner and the four of us all seemed to hit it off.

There was somebody else who had been watching me closely that weekend, a lovely gentleman called Dave More – a wheeler dealer from Guildford who loved a cash deal but was always way too generous with whatever he had worked so hard to earn. Dave also sponsored riders and he knew that if I was to get any real recognition I needed to be winning those bigger class races, so he offered to take his TZ750 Yamaha off his current rider and give it to me for the following year. It was a slightly awkward situation, especially when I had to tell Harold, who had helped me immensely. It was a case of: 'Thank you, but I've had a better offer.' To be honest, good old Harold had probably had enough of me smashing his bikes up anyway, and he understood my position, so we parted on good terms.

So Dave lent me his TZ750 Yamaha and off we went to Brands Hatch to debut it in a pretty important event, the Powerbike International, which would be televised on ITV – a rarity for motorcycle racing in the seventies, other than the odd clips of Barry that they showed on BBC's *Grandstand*. I would be taking part in one of the support class races, with the feature event set to include all the big names of the day: Barry, of course, and other riders I looked up to like Mick Grant, Barry Ditchburn and Dave Croxford. However, during the race there was a huge accident at Paddock Hill Bend and one of the top riders, Pat Mahoney, suffered severe injuries that he would sadly never fully recover from.

The race was red-flagged and it was chaos, with the television cameras still rolling and desperately needing to show something. The next scheduled race was ours and the organisers hurriedly brought it forward before ITV pulled the plug.

Before I knew it I was sitting on the grid aboard Dave More's 750 Yamaha for the first time in my life, ready to take part in a live televised race.

Nothing was expected of me because I had been riding smaller bikes for my whole career but somehow I went out there and won at the first attempt, beating established names like Percy Tait and a well-known Dutch rider called Boet van Dulmen. And, of course, with the race being shown live on television, all of a sudden everybody was talking about me.

The other slice of luck I had that season was meeting Martin Brookman. He would prove to be the greatest mechanic I ever worked with and I would happily have the pleasure of doing so for most of my career. Martin was from Wrestlingworth, the next village to me, and he worked for a local engineering business, where I used to go to get parts machined and re-paired. He was a pretty fearsome-looking fellow – 6' 6" tall and with hands like shovels that he wasn't afraid to use to give somebody a slap if they really annoyed him – but most of the time he was a lovely, placid person and just a hoarder of any-thing mechanical, who loved tinkering with whatever bits and pieces he could get his enormous hands on. I was getting him to help me out so much that I eventually asked him to come along to the races and he soon became an invaluable part of any success I had, working whatever hours it took to make the bike perfect and often even staying up right through the night before a race.

With Martin's priceless help, at the end of that season I won the Grosvenor Award and the Castrol Award for the Best Up and Coming Rider, which was the perfect start to my relation-ship with Dave More and even secured us some sponsorship from Castrol for the following season. I also picked up my first leather sponsorship deal, from this eccentric German called Brian Litler, who was the brains behind a new brand of leathers called Trim, which were made out of upper Mongolian goat skin or something, joined together by some kind of spandex. They were so bloody comfortable. I remember trying them on thinking 'These are the bollocks!' until I fell off the TZ750 in morning practice at Mallory Park, slid down the road at Gerard's and stood up in the middle of the track in nothing but my underpants. I had no skin all down my left side; it was down to the bone in places.

But by far the best thing about winning those awards at the end of 1975 was that I got invited to be a part of the British team in the Transatlantic Trophy Series for 1976, racing against the USA in a series of three events over Easter weekend: Good Friday at Brands Hatch, Easter Saturday at Mallory Park and Easter Monday at Oulton Park. There were only eight riders in each team, with me, Barry, Barry Ditchburn, Mick Grant, Phil Read, John Williams, Dave Potter and Ron Haslam representing Great Britain. I would be measuring myself not only against these guys but also against a new generation of American former flat-track stars who were revolutionising road racing at the time, including the aforementioned Kenny Roberts, Gene Romero, Steve Baker, Pat Hennen and Gary Nixon.

I was literally living my dream, although it quickly turned into a nightmare in the first race at Brands when I crashed and smashed the bike to bits for the umpteenth time that year. Dave had had the 750 modified, badly as it turned out, with a new frame that was bloody awful. It had a central spine running down the middle and I couldn't stay on the damned thing. Every time I crashed it would be in two pieces and I never quite knew if that had happened before or after I fell off it. Dave managed to borrow another one for the remaining two Transatlantic races but I couldn't really get going on it and over the three days it is fair to say that I didn't cover myself in glory. Worse still, the £2,000 starting fee, the first money I had ever been paid to race, had been soaked up by the bill for the repairs.

I crashed a lot back then, as a young rider does, but I was only in my early twenties so I bounced well. Dave's lovely wife Jan must have hated me. All she wanted was a new kitchen but I kept breaking his motorcycles, so he was spending all his hard-earned money on fixing them for me. Dave also splashed the cash on a brand-new Suzuki RG500, which was the ultimate racing machine. Out of the twenty or so that were made at the factory in Japan, Suzuki Great Britain were only given three or perhaps four to distribute in this country; I know Phil Read got one, I think Paul Smart got one, and on the back of those little awards I won at the end of 1975, Dave managed to secure one for me.

Unfortunately, just one of those precious bikes that came into the country had a manufacturing issue with the carburettor and, of course, it happened to be mine. We found out the hard way, on our first outing with it at the North West 200 races in Northern Ireland, in which I was competing for the first time. I was passing people with ease down those long, fast public roads between Portstewart, Coleraine and Portrush, and I reckon I would have won the race hands down but every time we went out the bike seized. Apart from that it was an incredible machine and as soon as Suzuki gave us a new carburettor I went on to win loads of races, culminating with the title in the British Open Motorcycle Championship, which was the main class.

Our success was also thanks in no small part to Martin Brookman, who proved his worth on more than one occasion that season. At one of the final meetings of the season I was fighting for the title with Roger Marshall, Ron Haslam, Steve Manship and Geoff Barry, when the ACU officials came around to check that we were running treaded tyres according to the regulations. In actual fact I had won my heat on a slick tyre, so unsurprisingly somebody lodged a protest, but before they had the chance to disqualify me Martin got the tyre cutter out and hastily cut some grooves in it. Then we persuaded the Dunlop guys to insist the cuts had been made back at the factory and somehow we managed to get away with it.

Also competing in some of those British Championship rounds were some of the top Grand Prix stars of the time, like Barry and his two factory Suzuki teammates, Jon Newbold and John Williams, as well as the likes of Jon Ekerold, Paul Smart and Phil Read. There were only eight Grands Prix per season back then, so those guys would probably come back to race ten events in Britain and other than Barry I usually smoked them all. It was a strange feeling, beating these guys I still looked up to so much. And as well as getting to spend a lot more time with Barry, I also became quite friendly with Phil Read, who even dropped by my house one Sunday afternoon in his Rolls-Royce Corniche.

Readie was a good-looking Luton boy with a massive talent for riding a motorcycle. Up until Valentino Rossi achieved the feat in 2001 he was the only guy to win the 125cc, 250cc and 500cc World Championships, and even though he was a boyhood hero of mine, and many other young racing fans, he never achieved the fame and recognition of somebody like Valentino or Barry Sheene in his day, simply because he didn't have the same charm. It's also fair to say that at times in his career he burned a few bridges. But when he rolled into Steeple Morden in his fancy car, it caused such a stir. The local ne'er do well was now rubbing shoulders with the rich and famous, don't you know! On a couple of occasions Readie even invited Linda and me down to stay with him at his beautiful nineteenth century thatched house in Oxshott in Surrey. It had eight bedrooms, a swimming pool, a gymnasium and massive garages all with brand-new Rollers in. As you can imagine, some pretty wild parties took place down there and I could hardly believe my luck that I was right in the thick of it.

I did a couple of international meetings that year too, including the opening two Grands Prix of the season in France and Austria, where I out-qualified Readie and led him in the race until I fell off. Barry had been keeping an eye on my progress as we had become close friends through all the time we were spending together in the British paddock and he badgered Suzuki to give me a chance in the factory Grand Prix team. It was partly because I was his mate, but also because I had proven I was faster than his two teammates, not to mention some of his main rivals for the World Championship.

I was aware that Barry was pushing for me but it wasn't until a letter arrived at my house, from Morris Knight at Suzuki Great Britain, that I knew for sure. I had to ring around my customers to tell them the news: I was jacking in Kerbside Motors to become a full-time motorcycle racer with the Texaco Heron Suzuki Grand Prix team.

4

Gas it wanker!

As far as I was concerned, life was about as good as it could get. I had just landed the best job in the world. Suzuki had the best team, Barry Sheene was the World Champion and one of the most famous men in the country and I was going to be his teammate, riding his title-winning bike from the previous year. As the current title holder Barry had the option to take the number 1 plate but he broke with tradition and stuck with his famous number 7. I took the number 6, and I would keep it for the rest of my career.

I guess Barry knew he had the beating of me. I would estimate I beat him ten times during my career and he beat me two hundred times. That's a good measure of how much better he was than me. He had more determination and certainly more self-belief than I ever had. So let's get that clear straight away: Barry was a winner and if he thought I was a threat to his success there is no way he would have been telling Suzuki to sign me up. Of course, I knew that, and quite frankly I didn't care.

I was still starstruck but since meeting Barry for the first time at that 'Stars of Tomorrow' event in 1974 I'd gelled with him a lot because it was the first time I had met anybody that I truly looked up to and respected. Up to that point I thought I knew it all but now I was in the company of somebody who was far more knowledgeable than me about the things I was really interested in. I truly admired him and now that we were friends he became the first person in my life that I could actually turn to for advice.

I would be the third rider in the factory-backed Texaco Heron Suzuki team, alongside Barry and Pat Hennen, who brought sponsorship from Suzuki USA. Pat was a methodical, meticulous man from Phoenix, Arizona and like his brother Chip he took his racing far more seriously than we did. He was similar in build to Barry and me, although I know for a fact he trained a lot harder, which may have been one of the reasons why Barry disliked him. The pair of them had already been teammates the previous season and had developed a huge rivalry both on and off the track, which now had me right in the middle of it.

My first appointment as a factory rider was to head down to Suzuki GB to get my pictures taken. I had to wear Barry's leathers because I obviously didn't have any made up, which as you can imagine was a bizarre experience. I was caught up in a whirlwind scenario where I went from one season racing Dave More's bikes in the national championship to suddenly being thrust into the limelight as one of the most high-profile motorcycle racers on the planet – on the front page of *Motor Cycle News* wearing the World Champion's leathers. To me and my mates down the Coach and Horses that was as big as it got: the newspaper I used to read about my heroes in, and now I was on the front page. It was unbelievable.

I was determined to prove to Suzuki that they had made the right choice and I put everything I had into getting the job right. I remember taking out the car ramps from the workshops and putting all my motorcycle equipment in there. My little repair business had been struggling anyway, because I had been spending so much time either away racing or preparing to go racing. When you start winning national races it's only natural to start thinking about the next step and now that moment had arrived. The next thing was to get my passport up to date and sort out a visa for the first round of the 1977 season, the Grand Prix of Venezuela.

The season started in Venezuela, I guess, because the weather was guaranteed to be better there in March than it was in Europe, where the remainder of the eleven-round championship would be held. The next round wouldn't take place until the start of May at Salzburgring in Austria, before we headed to Hockenheim (West Germany), Imola (Italy), Paul Ricard (France), Assen (the Netherlands), Spa-Francorchamps (Belgium), Anderstorp (Sweden), Imatra (Finland), Brno (Czech Republic) and, finally, home to Silverstone for the season finale in mid-August.

I had a test for a day or two at Snetterton and before I knew it I was on an aeroplane for the first time in my life, flying to Caracas with Barry and his new model girlfriend Stephanie McLean, who were very much the 'Posh and Becks' of the day. They were constantly surrounded by paparazzi and I would be getting shoved out of the way by photographers trying to get a closer snap, but I just hung in there in Barry's slipstream, soaking everything up. There wasn't quite the celebrity circus there is now because we lived in a smaller world and there was much less professional sport around, but Barry was definitely a mainstream celebrity and there are all sorts of photographs of me with him at these fancy functions, posing with famous footballers or cricketers, even though I had no idea who anybody was.

On arrival in Caracas we stayed in the big Tamanaco hotel and I was like a kid in a sweet shop, filling my suitcase with the soap, slippers and any other complimentary items that weren't bolted to the floor or walls, as you do when you go to a fancy hotel for the first time. I'd had a taste of the Grand Prix paddock the previous season when I rode in France and Austria but now I felt fully a part of what was quite literally a whole new world. I just loved meeting people from different countries who shared exactly the same interests, like Stuart Avant from New Zealand, Jack Findlay from Australia and Korky Ballington from South Africa – not to mention all the European guys – and learning about their backgrounds and cultures. It was a phenomenal experience.

The actual circuit at San Carlos, located in the middle of the desert with just a few tin shelters providing scant protection from the blazing sun, was primitive to say the least. Even in the shade the temperature was touching 50°C, so the conditions really were gruelling, with riders regularly passing out from heat exhaustion. Typically, Barry had worked out his own way to keep hydrated, by sucking on fresh limes rather than trusting the local water supplies, and he even befriended the local chief of police, who had a helicopter and would take us up to a lagoon to take a dip and cool off. We wondered why on earth he had brought a sheep with us until we arrived at the lagoon and they threw it into the water to check for crocodiles!

There were other hidden dangers at the track: rattlesnakes lying in the gravel traps provided an extra incentive not to crash, and on the gates of the compound an armed guard cocked his machine gun at Martin Brookman and me when we tried to get in early on the morning of the race. They had kicked everybody out at six o'clock the previous evening and we hadn't had time to fix a mechanical issue I'd had in practice, so we turned up at the crack of dawn; but this bloke had no intentions of letting us in. Martin had a serious temper and once got arrested in Finland for clouting a marshal who turned out to be a policeman but thankfully, on this occasion, he didn't argue.

Yet despite all these extra hazards – the volatile armed

guard, the debilitating heat, the crocodiles and the rattlesnakes – compared to some of the circuits I had been racing on back home like Cadwell Park or the Isle of Man this open expanse of track surrounded by nothing but sand still seemed like the safest place I had ever raced at.

I finished ninth in that first round in Venezuela and then took fourth place in my second race at Hockenheim in Germany behind Sheene, Hennen and Stevie Baker, a Canadian who rode for Yamaha USA. That was a typical result for that season; having to learn each track in practice, I would generally qualify terribly and then come on strong in the race. I threatened the podium on four or five occasions but I was never really in contention for a win because there were so many other established contenders with good bikes and prior experience of the circuits.

It's worth remembering too that most of these circuits were up to three times as long as current MotoGP tracks, so to try and learn them was hugely difficult. Of course, there were no games consoles or YouTube videos of on-board laps to learn from – you just turned up, had a walk or drive around and then off you went. Spa-Francorchamps in Belgium was nine miles long; it was like racing the TT with a huge section included that has since been removed, which wound its way through the local village. Annoyingly, on my first visit to Spa I finished one second back from the podium and just sixteen seconds behind Barry in a race that remains the fastest motorcycle Grand Prix ever held, with Sheenie clocking an average of 135.07mph. Present day MotoGP speeds, by comparison, average at around 109mph.

Part of the reason for that incredible average speed is the fact that Spa has a series of huge straights, where we were flat out and slipstreaming each other for miles at up to 185mph. I remember that race so well because I was in this fantastic battle with Hennen, Wil Hartog, a strong Finnish rider called Teuvo ('Tepi') Länsivuori, who had finished second in the championship to Barry in 1976, and the legendary fifteen-time 350cc and 500cc World Champion Giacomo Agostini, all passing each other back and forth down those never-ending straights. I can close my eyes now and picture myself pulling alongside Ago, thinking, 'I can't believe I am overtaking Giacomo Agostini!' and then seeing his blank expression looking back at me as if to say: 'Who the fuck are you?'

Clearly I didn't learn a lot at school but my new life was teaching me so much, on and off the track. And if the 1977 season was the equivalent of my university education then the ninth round of the season, the Finnish Grand Prix at Imatra, has to go down as my doctorate in explosives, courtesy of my great teacher Barry Sheene.

There were no garages in those days; everybody just had an awning pitched off the side of their van to keep the rain off their bikes. At Imatra the whole paddock was actually erected within a sports ground, right in the middle of this running track, beside which was a beautiful lake with a pretty shore. The lake was protected, so you couldn't have motorboats in it, just rowing boats, and even if you went for a swim you had to wear a swimming cap. The beauty of the lake was in stark contrast to the paddock facilities, which included an anti-quated little wooden toilet and shower block. Since it was only designed for a running club there were only a couple of stalls in the bogs, which always meant a long queue of riders about to shit themselves in the moments before the race. Imatra was one of the last remaining road races in the World Championship, composed of sections of closed-off public roads on the outskirts of the city that ran through a forest, beside the lake and even across a live train track. It was easily one of the scariest events on the calendar and definitely got the bowels moving.

But we loved going to Imatra because it never got dark in July and the girls and the alcohol came in equal supply. It was only when we had to actually race around that terrifying 3.747-mile circuit that the fun came to an abrupt halt. The thought of hitting a tree, house, lamppost or wall at 160mph was the perfect cure for a hangover, a night of passion, or both in most cases. Most circuits were dangerous and we accepted that, but there was no room for error or mechanical failure at Imatra. I would find myself wondering before the race whose caravan might get left behind when everybody else headed for the ferry that evening. Which one of us would be rushing to make that dreaded phone call back at the Valtinnen hotel, where just a few hours ago we'd been entertaining a bunch of blonde girls from Helsinki in the basement disco?

Your biggest fear had nothing to do with your ability or bravery on the bike because ninety-nine times out of a hundred a crash was out of your control. Highly-tuned two-stroke 500cc engines had a rather nasty habit of seizing at the wrong moment and in the wrong place, usually on the way into a corner. A two-stroke doesn't have any oil in the sump like a four-stroke – the lubricant is mixed in with the fuel, so when you shut the throttle you lose the lube. If the engine is set correctly it can survive for a short period of time but if you are running lean on fuel the expansion rate would quickly force it to seize and lock the rear wheel. Too rich and you lost performance.

We had a very simple means of testing the mixture, which we called a 'plug chop'. At the end of each practice session you would go flat out down the straight and then shut the throttle, pull the clutch in and stop the engine. It didn't matter if it seized in a straight line. At some circuits you could freewheel all the way back to your awning, otherwise you'd get off and push, or a truck would come along to tow everybody back. Then you'd have a look at the spark plugs: too white and it was

49

too lean, too black and it was too rich. The optimum setting produced a sandy colour. You would run it rich to start off with, so the engine wouldn't be running so fast in first practice, and then you'd work down from there. That kind of tuning has gone out of the window now but I was lucky to have such a good mechanic in Martin Brookman, and a decent amount of mechanical knowledge myself. Other riders, who chased extra speed by keeping the carburetion mix leaner, paid the price.

The first thing they'd know about it was usually when they were sliding down the track, their fate decided by what they did or didn't hit. Following somebody, you sometimes saw a little puff of smoke and that gave you a split second's warning to dodge out of the way. Very, very occasionally a sudden drop in revs would give you a tiny clue and the opportunity to whip in the clutch. It was like the Wild West out there, the riders like cowboys with one finger hovering over the clutch lever, often only finding out who was the quickest on the draw when it was too late. I still ride a modern-day road bike that way. Old habits die hard.

On that particular sunny Sunday evening at Imatra we were revelling not only in the usual euphoria of actually surviving a race like that but also because Barry's sixth place, one position behind me, had been enough to secure him the title for the second successive season. So as everybody else was packing up, we were feeling giddy. 'Stavros, that toilet block is an absolute joke,' Barry said. 'We need to get rid of it so that they have no choice but to put new bogs in for next year.' So we grabbed a can of Avgas and headed over to the toilets, checked nobody was inside and then Barry, being Barry, said: 'Right Stavros, you go inside and throw the Avgas everywhere, I'll stand out here and keep watch. When you come out, we'll light it.' So, of course, still as green as you like, I go in there and I'm tipping all the Avgas around, into the toilets and the showers, down the sinks and everywhere. I came out and it was all clear; everybody was still busy packing up their awnings and loading up their vans and caravans.

Now neither of us knew what methane gas was, but if we had known we would have stood a little further back as Barry pulled out a Gauloises, sparked it up and threw his lighter on the floor. 'BOOM!' The whole block was absolutely blown to smithereens; there were splinters of broken timber, debris and human shit blown high into the air and across the whole paddock, while the roof landed upside down in a ball of flames in the middle of the lake. They didn't want dirty engines or even human hair in the water but now they had a shithouse roof that was on fire! Barry and I looked at each other, both covered head to toe in human faeces and now quite literally in the middle of another massive shitstorm, as Korky Ballington, Jon Ekerold and Tom Herron led a lynch mob of angry riders hunting down the culprits.

We almost ended up in the shit again that year in a post-Isle of Man TT meeting at Mallory Park. Barry came in after first free practice and he had a problem with his knee, which he had broken in a huge crash that almost cost him his life at Daytona in 1975. It would later turn out that one of the screws in his famous bionic leg had come loose, but his whole knee locked up and they couldn't get him fixed in time for qualifying. There was only one way to make sure he was on the grid for the race, and as usual I was willing to go along with the plan.

Unlike nowadays, when you turn up Thursday, practise Friday, qualify Saturday and race on Sunday, these meetings used to take place all on one day. There was no time to waste so Franco, Barry's dad, bundled Barry up under a blanket in the back of his Rolls-Royce and took him down to a local chiropractor, who worked the screw and got his joint moving again. Meanwhile, back at the track, it was all arranged for me to put Barry's leathers and helmet on, jump on the number 7 bike and complete the mandatory three laps to set a qualifying time. It didn't really matter how fast I was, as long as I got Barry on the grid for the race.

It felt pretty cool to be out there, living every kid's dream with the famous number 7 on my back and Barry's helmet on. I did three quick laps with the crowd cheering me on and the girls waving their knickers, whipped straight back into the pit, parked the bike up in the awning and disappeared out of the back. Within minutes there was a gaggle of journalists surrounding the awning, wanting to know why Barry had pulled in and whether there was a problem with the bike. The mechanics gave them some story about a disc valve malfunction, by which time I was already back in my caravan, changing into my own leathers and helmet.

Out I went again, this time on my number 6 bike, with about twenty minutes left of the session. I must have done six laps before I came back in, made some adjustments to the suspension, went back out for another six laps, came in, changed the gearing, went out for another five laps; and that was the end of my session. Barry gets back to the track and says: 'Stavros, how'd it go?' I said: 'I don't know mate, but it should be okay. I did three laps for you and about twenty for myself. I reckon it will be fine.'

Again unlike nowadays, there were no fancy digital timing systems or transponders on the bikes. The lap times were clocked by four ladies in the control tower with stopwatches and it wasn't until a couple of hours later that the qualifying classification was posted on a noticeboard. I couldn't believe it: I'd managed to qualify myself on the second row and Barry on the front row! I'm still not sure what went on there, but I can only assume it was either a better bike or the girls waving their knickers that made me go faster.

I didn't know it at the time but that whole 1977 season would prove to be the highlight of my motorcycle racing career. I was riding for a full factory effort with the reigning World Champion as teammate, who was now also my best friend, and I was having the time of my life. I was racing against true legends like Giacomo Agostini, Phil Read and all these huge superstars of the sport, and by the time it got to the final round, my home Grand Prix at Silverstone, I was pretty satisfied with my season. I still had a good chance of finishing third in the World Championship, which would have been pretty good for my first year, and most importantly for the team and the factory, of course, Barry had already won the title.

It was a special year for the British Grand Prix because it had been moved to Silverstone from the Isle of Man, after pressure and increased boycotts from some of the top riders, including Agostini, who felt the TT circuit was too dangerous for a World Championship race. With Sheenie celebrating his second straight championship there and it being the final round of the season, there was sure to be a huge crowd and a party atmosphere at Silverstone. However, Barry was having all sorts of problems in practice: the head gasket kept going on his Suzuki, which was a newer version than mine, so he ended up using my bike to set pole position. Thanks, as always, to Martin my bike was running so sweet that weekend and after qualifying fourth I was really fired up for the race, which I felt I might even have a chance of winning. At least, I felt, I could give Barry a proper race, although that possibility would evaporate on the ninth lap when his bike broke down for the final time that season.

It was a 22-lap race and the first few laps had been tough but I always liked Silverstone whenever I rode it on a 250 or 350 and the fast, flowing nature of the track lent itself even more to the more powerful 500cc machine. As a huge former RAF airfield, Silverstone was also much wider and safer than the circuits we were used to and this suited my self-preservationist leanings, giving me the confidence to come out on top of a tremendous scrap with Länsivuori in the early stages and then overcome the challenge of Williams, Hartog, Hennen, Agostini and Johnny Cecotto to lead with about five laps to go.

With their idol Barry back on the pit wall, the crowd had a new hero to cheer along: little old me, carrying British hopes of a home winner in the first ever British Grand Prix to be held at Silverstone on my shoulders. The chance of making this kind of history would have been way beyond my wildest dreams just twelve months earlier, yet here I was, leading all these famous names on my way to victory in my home round at the first attempt.

If you watch modern-day motorcycle or F1 racing you'll know that the pit boards are made from fancy aluminium frames. Individual numbers, letters, names and even codes printed on square pieces of plastic are slotted into the frame, which the mechanic will then hang over the pit wall to transmit information to the rider as he comes past. The team will be watching the live timing screens and will often not adjust the board until just before the final sector, to give the riders the most accurate and up-to-date information possible. In 1977 we just had a stopwatch and a chalkboard and I counted the last five laps down one by one, as Martin leaned over and literally chalked them off.

With two laps to go the board read 'L2 Williams +3.0', meaning I had a three-second advantage over John Williams, the man in second place, and as I came through Woodcote for the penultimate time I glanced over my shoulder to check he was still there before I started that final, triumphant lap. My RG500 Suzuki seemed to be enjoying the moment as much as I was. For all the troubles that Barry was having with this year's model, the bike he had won on the previous season had not missed a beat all weekend and now it was ready for its glorious swansong.

My first-ever race bike: a Triton Hybrid that dropped its guts all over Brands Hatch. I'm convinced the circuit is still slippery today because of that bloody bike. (Chris Morgan)

Barry Sheene and our great friend Piers Weld-Forrester, an adrenaline-junkie aristocrat who somehow persuaded me to join him at the British Olympic bobsleigh trials. (CSS)

The first proper team I ever rode for: the Coppock Superchicks. With my team-mates Wayne Dinham (left) and Mick Patrick (right) and team owner Harold Coppock, a wealthy chicken farmer and motorcycle-racing philanthropist.

Above: In 1975 I signed for Dave More and, even though I did a lot of damage to his bikes, our success together persuaded Suzuki to provide us with one of the only RG500s to come in to the country. (Keith Wigmore)

We won the British Open Motorcycle Championship on it in 1976 and, with a little push from my new best mate Barry Sheene, the door to the World Championship creaked open.

Barry persuaded Texaco Heron Suzuki to sign me for 1977, and I could hardly believe my luck.

Here I am with my girlfriend Linda at the photoshoot to announce the deal. I had to wear my hero's leathers because mine weren't ready yet. I was literally living the dream.

In between my Texaco Heron Suzuki team-mates Pat Hennen and Barry Sheene, as well as Phil Read on a borrowed Kawasaki at Brands Hatch in 1977.

Above: I suddenly found myself amongst other sporting stars that I'd never even heard of. You might recognise me here with TV presenter Dickie Davies, footballer Malcolm Macdonald, and England cricket captain Mike Brearley, although I still have no idea which is which. (LAT)

Right: Leading my home Grand Prix at Silverstone in my first full season as a World Championship rider, running the number 1 on my bike. By the end of the race I would be the number 1 wanker.

Rolling up to the starting grid at Imatra, Finland, in 1979. The locals had me to thank for the new toilet block, although curiously there is no plaque there in my honour.

Linda and Steph Sheene, Italy, 1980. How bloody fast?! (Richard McLaren/DPA)

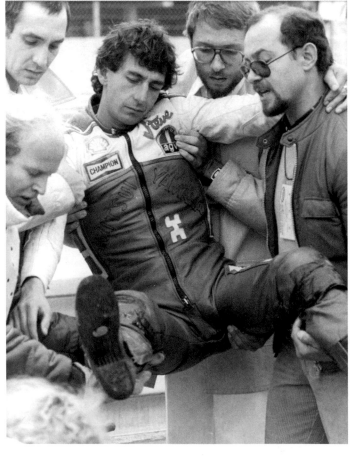

Being team-mate to Barry Sheene was everything you'd expect. Here we are on one of our regular pre-season 'training' excursions to Venezuela, which consisted mainly of waterskiing and sampling the local 'delights'.

Hockenheim, 1982. Broken leg and ankle. Whatever happened to stretchers?

Probably the closest I ever came to losing my life on a racetrack was when I crashed and Kenny Roberts ran over my head at the Transatlantic Challenge meeting at Donington Park in 1984. Randy Mamola was also caught up in the incident and the pair of them helped the medics to carry me away in a blanket. They both feared the worst and the look in Barry's eyes as he came around on the next lap tells the story.

I had my share of flash cars over the years but soon found out that novelty vehicles were far more fun. Over the years I owned an ambulance, an armoured vehicle, a fire engine and a hearse. But my favourite was my 'Trotters Independent Trading' three-wheeler.

Barry was my best man, my best friend and the person I looked up to most in the world. 'Never die wondering,' he used to say. He didn't, and I am determined that I won't either. (LAT)

With Williams three seconds behind me and a place in history just two minutes ahead of me, I prepared to put my head down for the remaining three miles of a race that would surely go down in the annals. However, the final moments turned out to be something that sounds very similar to annals, but couldn't be more different. For hanging over the pit wall at the start of that final lap was not Martin Brookman but Barry Sheene, with a big grin on his face and a pit board that said 'LL P1' – meaning last lap, position one – and below it three more, immortal words in bold, white chalk: 'Gas it wanker!'

I couldn't help but smirk to myself. I mean, it was bloody funny. In the grandstands the crowd went wild as I roared down the main straight and my smirk grew wider because I knew this was nothing compared to what the reaction would be like when I came back round again the next time. The banners and the Union flags were flying in anticipation of a party to end all parties and at last this time it would be me, Stephen J. Parrish from Church Farm, Steeple Morden, as the centre of attention.

What I didn't know was that on the other side of the track the stands were also buzzing with activity, as people started dropping their flags and rummaging around in their bags for umbrellas and raincoats. The weather can come in quickly at that big, flat expanse of Northamptonshire land and as I started to brake from 150mph to 90mph on my way into turn one at Copse, a few splodges of water splashed against my visor. Nowadays racers call it 'mental rain', as your brain starts to send mixed messages to your body about how to respond to the changing track conditions. Sadly, I never had the opportunity to respond at all.

Before I knew it, I was watching that beautiful, reliable Suzuki dismantling itself into several pieces as it skidded and scraped towards the catch fence, with me sliding helplessly along behind it on my backside. I finally came to a halt underneath one of the few hay bales Silverstone had in those days and I spent a few moments in the silent pitch blackness wondering if I had actually died, before a kind marshal came and extracted me. Sadly, there was no saving my poor bike; with a broken brake lever, a snapped footrest and bent handlebars, I knew there was nothing left for me to salvage from that cursed afternoon.

John Williams' dream ended in exactly the same fashion at Becketts, two corners later, leaving my bloody teammate Pat Hennen to claim his first victory of the season and spark the celebrations that were supposed to be for me back in the Texaco Heron Suzuki pits. The rain grew heavier with my mood as I trudged back through the paddock to the team awning, where I was greeted by an even damper reception. Even Barry was struggling to look on the bright side. 'For God's sake, Stavros,' he scolded me. 'How could you let that American prat win?'

A week or so later, less than twelve months since that dream letter from Suzuki had dropped through my letterbox, another one landed on the mat to tell me that I'd been fired. Suzuki were cutting back the factory team to two riders for the following season and due to the fact that he finished above me on championship points, by way of his victory at Silverstone, they were duty-bound to keep Hennen.

It was pretty brutal but it was the way business was conducted back then and as a racer you knew you were only ever as good as your last race. Either way, it was a rubbish end to an otherwise great year and even now I'm not sure whether it was down to the rain, the pit board or just me genuinely being a wanker, but I certainly couldn't blame Barry. It was him that got me the ride in the first place and, remarkably, it would be thanks to him and his friendship with a member of the most famous rock band in the world that I made it back to the Grand Prix circus for the following season.

5

A little help from my friends

By 1977, The Beatles had long since gone their separate ways and while Paul McCartney was enjoying great success with Wings, John Lennon had disappeared up his own arse with Yoko Ono and nobody really gave a shit what Ringo Starr was up to. George Harrison, though, was a real petrol head. Barry had met him on the London scene and would often invite him to hang out at the circuits and watch us race. In turn, George would invite us down to Friar Park, his house in Henley-on-Thames, and we got to hang out there with other well-known celebrities of the time, like Eric Idle from Monty Python. I always remember George had a great love of gardens and his place in Henley was absolutely stunning, with a cave in it full of stalactites and stalagmites. He also had a huge garage, lined up with all kinds of exotic Ferraris and Porsches.

George was such a gentle guy who had so much admiration for us and what we did, although he didn't think much of us as singers. On one occasion he invited us down to his studio to sing on the backing track of a song he had written about motor racing called 'Faster'. Sadly, no amount of knob twiddling on that big desk of his was enough to convince him that we could become singers, any more than he could become a racer, and even though I felt I had mastered the triangle by the time we finished we all agreed to stick to our day jobs, if that's what you could call them.

So when I got fired by Suzuki, George said in his gentle Liverpudlian way: 'Ah, don't worry our Stavros, I'll buy you a few tyres and cover your fuel and that so you can keep racing.' Sure enough, later that winter I got a message telling me to head down to the offices of Dark Horse Records and Harrisongs in Sloane Square, where a very smart, prim and proper lady handed me a cheque, written out by the record label, for £50,000. 'You are the third person this week and it's only Tuesday!' she smiled, shaking her head. George was a great supporter of numerous causes and I was lucky to be one of the chosen ones.

I must admit I wasn't into The Beatles as such, but then I wasn't really much into music. I was ignorant of it and still am. A few years ago, somebody bought me a CD by a band called Razorlight, which I really liked and listened to constantly in the car. One day while out shopping with my girlfriend Michelle I wandered into a record store and heard a song over the speakers that I liked the sound of, so I asked an assistant if I could buy whatever CD was playing. That was the first and only CD I ever bought, so I now have two copies of Razorlight's album, if anybody wants one.

However, you don't need to be into music to know who The Beatles are, so having the world-famous George Harrison as my sponsor was hugely exciting – not least because it opened lots of doors to other potential sponsors who wanted to associate themselves with George's name. One of them was Makaha skateboards, who had been riding the crest of a skateboarding craze during the mid-seventies. They had wanted to sponsor Barry initially but Suzuki wouldn't let him do it, so the deal was slid my way by his management company, CSS. God knows how much of the money actually trickled down to me, but I wasn't complaining because it was still a decent amount and it seemed a good deal to me, apart from injuring myself whenever I tried to get on one of their bloody skateboards! Unfortunately for Makaha, their move into motorcycle sponsorship coincided with a downturn in the skateboard business and they went broke before the end of 1978, thankfully not before covering the terms of our deal.

Barry wasn't daft. He knew that rich people wanted to look cool by hanging out with him and his famous friends, which in turn allowed him to meet potential sponsors from all manner of industries. Of course, he loved the party life but he was also a shrewd businessman; he knew how to market himself and he never stopped working. He started to move in the same circles as advertising agency executives and got introduced to top brass from the likes of Fabergé, Marlboro cigarettes or Mash jeans, who all became his sponsors at one time or another. When you look back at pictures from that era, every other rider is sponsored by Shell Oils, Dunlop tyres, Ferodo brake pads and Renold chains. In this respect Barry was a true pioneer and the benefits of the glamour he first brought to our sport are still being felt to this day.

And as well as cash for sponsorship Barry was also inundated with freebies and special discounts, which seemed just as important. As soon as you were seen in the magazines hanging out with George Harrison at Tramp nightclub, you almost didn't need money because you had everything thrown at you for nothing.

I remember one such freebie that was given to him in 1980: a brand-new, top-of-the-range Ford Granada, fully specced up with air conditioning, leather seats and everything else. Barry had just had a new speedboat built called *My Doreen*, which was an affectionate nickname he gave to Stephanie whenever she was doing the housework. It was February, it was absolutely freezing and Barry had his hand all bandaged up because he'd just had his finger amputated, having injured it beyond repair in a crash at Paul Ricard some months earlier; but he was so keen to get this boat on the water we used the new Granada to tow it down to Shoreham Harbour, near Brighton. He could drive the car okay, but when we got down there he said: 'Look Stavros, whatever happens I can't get this bandage wet so you're going to have to unhitch the boat while I drive the car.'

So I got out in readiness for him to back down the slipway and ease the boat into the water. With it being winter, together with the obvious fact that nobody in their right mind had been using it at that time of year, the slipway was covered in slime and as soon as he backed onto it the whole lot – boat, trailer, car and all – started sliding into the water. Barry started to panic. 'Stavros!!' he's shouting, holding his hand up out of the window as the water started to flood into the boot and the back seats: 'Get the fucking trailer off!' But the trailer was already under and the boat was now afloat, dragging the car with it out to sea. I was in jeans and an anorak but I had no choice but to dive in, taking deep breaths and plunging underwater to try and unhook this bloody trailer. It had electric wires on it and safety cables and I was under there fiddling about with my eyes closed in the freezing water until finally I managed to release it. As I came up gulping for air, hanging onto the side of the boat, it drifted out into the harbour with the trailer still attached to the bottom.

Despite the freezing temperature it was actually a nice sunny day and there were a few people down at Shoreham cleaning their boats and pootling around the harbour. They seemed to think I was doing this on purpose so they were waving and nodding at me, with me waving back saying 'Good afternoon!' as if this was totally normal, while kicking away frantically under the water in my jeans and trainers. Meanwhile Sheenie's spinning up the wheels of the Granada on the boat ramp, trying to haul it back onto dry land. Eventually somebody realised we were actually in quite a lot of trouble and got a tractor to drag us out, by which time the car was a complete write-off. He'd only had it three days!

Although we never saw the Granada again, Barry's amputated finger did make one more appearance. The sneaky bugger had preserved it in a jar of vinegar and one Sunday afternoon he invited me and my girlfriend Linda round for a full roast dinner, as he often did back then, with Stephanie, Barry's sister Maggie and her husband Paul Smart. As usual everything between us turned into a competition and we were just about to start a race to see who could eat the most Yorkshire puddings when I moved a slice of beef to the side of my plate and revealed his finger, complete with a yellow nail on it. Barry could barely swallow for laughing as he ploughed his way through his pile of Yorkshires, which I, of course, could no longer face. You could say that was another under-handed victory for Sheene!

Anyway, in those days fifty grand was a serious amount of money, enough to buy you a detached house in a nice area, so with the cheque George gave me and the extra sponsorship I gained just by having the Harrison name on the side of my bike, I actually ended up with more cash coming in than I had earned the previous season as a factory rider with Texaco Heron Suzuki. It was certainly more than enough to put a strong motorcycle racing team together and that's exactly what I did. I bought a TZ750 Yamaha and a couple of Suzukis, then hired Martin Brookman, and even though I wasn't officially a Suzuki rider any more they agreed to help me out with spare parts and I still travelled with Barry and all our other mechanics.

Our preseason training programme was to go to Venezuela on 1 January and with sponsorship from British Caledonian Airways we helped several members of their cabin crew join the 'mile high club' on the way, including one poor girl who got the sack as a result. Apparently she got grassed up by the purser, who I guess must have been jealous. Once we were back on the ground our exercise routine was limited mainly to waterskiing, which we would do pretty much every day for a month. As usual it would turn into another competition, with Steph as official photographer and Barry judging the winner by using a protractor to measure the lean angle.

Venezuela produced a bunch of top-class racers in the 1970s, probably because a lot of motorcycles were being sold in that country at the time. There was a huge distributor called Venemotos, which was owned by Andrea Ippolito, whose son Vito went on (until quite recently) to become president of the FIM. Mr Ippolito was the founder of the Latin American Motorcycle Union and the Venezuelan importer for Yamaha, who sold hundreds of thousands of bikes down there, so I guess even though they didn't have a lot of tracks or anything, they got a lot of help to bring riders through to Grand Prix racing – the likes of Carlos Lavado, Roberto Pietri and Johnny Cecotto.

Johnny was a cool, olive-skinned South American dude with thick black hair and an enormous natural talent for riding a motorcycle fast, who became the youngest rider ever to win a World Championship when he claimed the 350cc title in 1975, aged 19. He was as smooth off the track as he was on it and even though he spoke very little English Barry spoke enough Spanish for the two of us and we always found a way of communicating once we had a few drinks inside us.

Johnny was a factory man from very early on and he was such a talent that he even went on to drive in Formula 1, before becoming a very successful touring car driver. Pietri also became a particularly good friend of ours and with his natural charm and the twinkle of mischief in his eye he easily talked us into visiting his home country for a holiday. He knew of this incredible resort with a hotel right on the beach in a place called Tucacas on the northern coast. The place was like a stunning nature reserve, free of tourists, where the jetsetters of Caracas would go for a short break. We'd go out on a boat every day, waterskiing and fishing, our long, exhausting days on the water often boosted by some of the local 'natural products' that were readily available.

On one occasion in Venezuela we took Stephanie and Linda along and we were all feeling a little jet-lagged, so we threw the anchor out while we had an afternoon siesta on the boat. A short time later we were woken up by a massive jolt, accompanied by the almighty crashing and scraping sound of the boat smashing itself against the rocks. It turned out that the anchor hadn't been tied to the deck, so not only had we fucked the boat but we'd also lost the anchor! On another occasion we forgot to pull the anchor back in and when we set off it grabbed so hard on a rock that it came flying out of the sea, skimmed over our heads and smashed into the front end of the boat. If that thing had hit any of us it would have killed us for sure.

As well as assisting our preseason campaign, our connections in Venezuela also came in useful when we went back there in March 1978 for the first race of the new season. When all the freight arrived at a warehouse at Caracas airport, before being loaded onto trucks to take it down to the track in San Carlos, Barry gave the warehouse staff 200 bolivars, the equivalent of about twenty quid, to hide all the crates with Yamaha stickers on them. So the trucks departed for the track leaving Kenny Roberts' bikes behind! Eventually, I imagine, the Yamaha boys had to hand over a similar bung to dig them out, but the crates were two days late arriving at the track and only just made it in time for practice. I don't know if that had anything to do with it but Kenny, who was making his debut in the 500cc World Championship that weekend, broke down with a mechanical issue in the race, although he went on to have the last laugh by winning the title by ten points in an incredible rookie season.

For me, the 1978 campaign was a solid one, with a couple of top five Grand Prix finishes and a close battle for the 500cc Shell Sport British Championship, which I was leading going into the final round at Brands Hatch, where my bike packed in and I handed the title to Barry. That would have been a special title for me because it would have been the first time I had contested the same number of rounds as Barry, on virtually the same bike too. But I did win the ACU 'Gold Star' Championship, which was the less prestigious open class, for bikes up to 750cc, and with Pat Hennen sadly suffering a career-ending crash at the TT earlier that summer I was offered the chance to return to Suzuki in 1979 alongside Barry and Tom Herron, who ironically had been battling with Pat at the TT when he crashed. It would prove to be another tragic year for the team. Barry didn't have a good season and would end up falling out with Suzuki as a result, I broke my wrist at the first round in Venezuela and far, far worse than all of that was Tom's death at the North West 200 in the May. Tom and I were actually battling with each other for third place as we went into Juniper Hill, the final bend. There were a few spots of rain around but Tom tried to go around the outside of me and out of the corner of my eye I saw the treaded tyre of his front wheel edging closer. I was on this very narrow dry line and the rest of the road was damp or even wet. I remember I looked over and thought: 'What the fuck are you doing there?' A fraction of a second later Tom's wheel disappeared and he was gone too.

That awful day will always be remembered as 'Black Saturday', as it also claimed the lives of two other riders: a Scotsman called Brian Hamilton and a Northern Irishman called Frank Kennedy. But by then death at the racetrack was nothing new to me and I had already lost seven or eight good mates while racing. Steve Machin, with whom I shared a garage at the Southern 100, died at Cadwell in 1974. Then there was Mick Patrick, my Coppock Superchicks teammate from 1974, who died at Cadwell Park in 1977, shortly before Piers Weld-Forester. My pal Norman Tricoglus was one of four guys killed in the 1977 Manx TT, while Mac Hobson was one of five to go at the TT the following year. We also lost Geoff Barry at the North West 200 in 1977 and John Williams at the Ulster Grand Prix in 1978. I was there for all of them.

I remember having to drive Mick Patrick's wife Vivienne home from Cadwell and passing the haunting image of their caravan, standing alone in an otherwise empty paddock, as we left. It would become a familiar scene that always hit home for me more than the accident. You could easily forget a guy who wasn't there any more, but there was no getting away from what he left behind. As the years passed there would be many others: Dave Potter, Patrick Pons, Michel Rougerie, Jock Taylor, John Newbold, Bob Smith, Norman Brown, Michel Frutschi, Kevin Wrettom and Mark Salle, to name but a few. Some were close friends, others not necessarily so, but I might have seen them in the shower block that morning or shared a cup of tea. In motorcycle racing there was a tremendous amount of respect and camaraderie but to me there was also always a point where the friendship stopped. For one thing we had to race each other, but guys were also disappearing at a quite alarming rate. I suppose we developed an in-built suppressor to stop us really getting into each other's pockets.

65

Why did we keep racing? We were having so much fun that whatever the risk was it seemed worth it. It wasn't just the buzz of racing but the whole lifestyle that came with it. There was no way of experiencing that by living my life in any other way. I felt then and I feel now that if I didn't have that kind of excitement going on I might as well be dead anyway.

Maybe it was a self-preservationist mindset, and in black and white it reads horribly, but when a competitor did die my thought process would be: 'Well, at least I'm not going to have to race him any more.' My competitive, single-minded nature actually overpowered any real feelings of grief. I had been looking after myself from the age of 12 and my first thought in any situation has always been: 'How will this make a difference to me?' When I heard Tom Herron had died, on the radio in the van on the way back to the ferry at Larne with Martin, my first thought was whether we might get a better engine from Suzuki for the next race. It is completely selfish, I know, but the truth is every successful sportsperson has an element of that egotism about them and I don't think they're telling the truth if they say otherwise.

Barry and I had a rule that we never went to funerals but Suzuki asked me if I would please go to Tom's on their behalf. So I flew over to Belfast, picked up a hire car and drove up to where the funeral was going to be. I got to within about three miles of the church and I couldn't go any further. I didn't mean any disrespect to Tom, I just didn't feel that I could be there at his funeral and then go out and race my bike the next weekend.

Barry and I did go back to Ireland for a memorial event at a place just outside Belfast later that year. It was right in the middle of the troubles there and we were met at the steps of the aeroplane by an armoured army vehicle, known as a 'Humber Pig', and taken to this large complex around twenty miles from the airport. The organisers gave us a room and it seemed to me that of the hundreds of people who had turned up, most of them were girls looking to meet Barry. Being a good mate, I managed to step in for him and do my little bit to help smooth out the otherwise fraught Anglo-Irish relationships of the time.

I can't take all the credit, of course, but it's great that English racers can head to modern events like the Ulster Grand Prix and the North West 200 and not worry about safety until they get on their motorcycles, although it wasn't always the case. I remember going to the UGP in the late seventies with Stuart Avant, a Kiwi racer who came to stay at my house for a week and ended up stopping for eight months, and when we went to check into the hotel they told us our room had gone. I said: 'It can't have gone, I booked it months ago and have the reservation number and everything.' But it turned out a whole wing of the hotel had been blown up by the IRA, so we had to sleep in the van. It wasn't so bad for the North West, which is right up out of the way in Coleraine, but for the Ulster we were right on the outskirts of Belfast and we had to be very careful about which parts of the city we visited.

Despite all this danger, I have to say the risk of racing motorcycles never really registered with me. I fell off my bike, bounced, got up and got on with it. I never thought anything bad could happen. You had to tell yourself that if anybody was going to die that day, it would be somebody else and not you. I guess if you worked in a factory and a bloke had a pallet dropped on his head, it wouldn't stop you from going in the next day. You'd be more likely to think, 'Well, that can't happen again', and be glad that the odds were now somehow stacked more in your favour. Back then, you knew that of all the guys you started a season racing with, two or three would disappear before the end of the year. And each time one person died you felt as if there was less likelihood of it happening to you. It's a strange logic, but it is one way of explaining how we were able to just carry on.

That was my mindset anyway, although I'm quite sure a few others dealt with it by taking a swig of Dutch courage before a race. I know an Italian racer called Guido Paci certainly did. He was one of the first riders to have a motorhome rather than a caravan and I remember walking past it on my way to the starting grid at the Imola 200 in 1983, when I saw him sitting with his girlfriend in the window. He held up a tumbler of whisky and said, 'Want one of these, Steve?' as if it was totally normal. I politely declined, of course. Personally, I didn't think more courage was a very wise thing to have when doing such a dangerous pursuit. Sure enough, after a few laps the yellow flags came out and when I was queuing up to collect my start money at the end of the race, word came back that it had been Paci.

In many ways it was harder for the wives and girlfriends than it was for the riders. The ladies really all stuck together and looked after each other when something went wrong. The guys just blanked it out and kept on moving forwards, but I think over time there is no way that it can't affect you and it is normal that we all became different people as a result. I guess at the bottom of our stomachs we knew full well that any one of us could be next. So as far as Barry and I were concerned, we devoted our lives to having as much fun as we possibly could.

And there was nobody better at that than us!

6

Never die wondering

'Never die wondering.' That was Barry's motto and we lived by it every day. I certainly didn't have to wonder how flight-loads of hostesses might spend each evening at the Gatwick Penta Hotel, which was conveniently located just down the road from Barry and Steph's beautiful new manor house in Charlwood.

The number one airline as far as I was concerned was undoubtedly Air Florida, who were based in Miami. Their policy at the time was only to employ tall blonde girls under the age of 25, so every evening at 5.30 p.m. around twenty or so young 5' 11" blondes would walk straight off their flight from Miami and into the hotel bar, giggly as hell and looking for a good time during their 12 hours off. It seemed my duty as a patriotic British man to once again take diplomatic measures into my own hands, this time in the interests of Anglo-US relationships. It may have only taken a couple of minutes, but I believe those girls got to see the very best sights London had to offer.

Luckily for me, just when it started to become a little too expensive to keep hiring a room at the hotel I got sponsored by a building supplies company, who used to loan me a caravan every year for my racing. Of course, I needed somewhere to park it up during the winter so it made perfect sense to keep it in the hotel car park. I just had to make sure I adjusted the jacks on a fairly regular basis.

We truly felt like we could get away with anything and it was while Barry was living down in Charlwood that we really put this to the test, with a feat of outlawry to make Robin Hood himself proud. Stephanie had a housekeeper at the time called Sarah, who was a cheerful girl with a rather overactive knife and fork. Sarah had recently started dating a new boy-friend and without wanting to sound mean to her it was fairly obvious that she was punching above her not inconsiderable weight. Sure enough, it turned out the lad was taking her for a ride and before long he had conned her out of £250.

The poor girl came into work in tears because the money was all she could afford, and now this slimeball had broken up with her and disappeared with it. Stephanie told Barry, who was absolutely furious, and when I arrived later that evening to stay for a couple of nights, as I did most weeks, he said: 'Right Stavros, we've got a job on tonight!' Somehow he'd managed to get hold of this guy's address in Crawley and had spent all afternoon hatching a plan to get the money back. When I say 'plan', what I actually mean is a burglary.

Sarah had told Barry that the bloke went football training on a Thursday night and always went out for a couple of beers afterwards. So we taped up the number plates on my car, drove over to his house and parked up around the corner. After slipping our balaclavas on we crept quietly up the path, smashed one of the little window panes on the front door and let ourselves into the house. We took a Bang & Olufsen stereo, a microwave, a shotgun, a few other bits and bobs and any cash that was lying around and then raced back to Charlwood, pissing ourselves with laughter the whole way.

I chipped a hundred quid in for the stereo, we sold the

microwave to a mechanic of mine called Dave Johnson and the shotgun and the other bits and bobs went off elsewhere, until we had totalled up £250 to give back to Sarah. Remarkably, almost forty years later, Dave recently sent me a message saying that the microwave is still going strong; and the B&O stereo is still in my little gym at home! It still brings a smile to my face whenever I look at it. Can you imagine one of the country's biggest sports stars doing something like that now? It's quite extraordinary really, but it just seemed normal to us. And in all honesty, I think if the police had caught us and Barry had pulled his balaclava up, they'd have let us go with a slap on the back and we'd have ridden off into the glen!

Our extra-curricular adventures extended further afield when Barry learned to fly a helicopter down at Shoreham, near Brighton. Being who he was, of course, he got to know all the air traffic controllers at Gatwick Airport and pretty much had carte blanche to fly through their airspace whenever he wanted. So we used to fly backwards and forwards down to Brighton all the time; mainly because, before the days of GPS, it was easy to find, because we could follow the train line all the way from Gatwick. But also there just happened to be a nudist beach there, which we discovered was best viewed from a helicopter. We certainly saw sand in some unusual places and got a few things standing to attention!

Unlike any other pilot who has to radio in to air traffic control and adhere to the recognised code of terms and abbreviations, such as VFR for 'visual flight rules' or ILS for 'instrument landing system', Barry had come up with his own way of communicating with the guys, and especially girls, at Gatwick. So whereas normal procedure would have been something like, 'Good afternoon, Gatwick, this is Golf Bravo Mike Golf X-ray, Enstrom helicopter requesting VFR transit through your overhead', Barry would just say in his chirpy

Cockney accent: 'Good morning guys, Barry here! Alright to come through?' Sure enough the reply would come back: 'Oh, morning Barry! Sure, come on through.'

However, on one occasion the reply that came back was slightly different. 'Good morning Golf Bravo Mike Golf X-ray, we can see you are six miles south of the field. We have an Air Florida 747 on the ILS for runway twenty-five. Please make a right-hand orbit until he is clear and then we will clear you for a VFR overhead not above fifteen hundred feet.' We'd obviously intruded at a busy time, and as we came in over the runway we could see the Air Florida flight full of all those lovely air hostesses coming in on one side, as well as a British Caledonian flight leaving on the other. Just then there was an almighty clattering sound from immediately outside. Barry grabbed the radio again: 'Mayday! Mayday! It's Barry here and the bloody helicopter is falling to pieces!'

Within seconds we heard air traffic control make an urgent appeal to the other aircraft. 'Gatwick N272 to Air Florida, please turn right immediately, abort landing!' So the 747 banked right and headed off towards Brighton, before further instructions were issued to the flights coming in behind to enter a holding pattern. While we were causing absolute pandemonium in the air around us, Barry had managed to stay calm enough to autorotate the helicopter to the ground and land it, right on the edge of the main runway.

We could see there were fire engines and ambulances dispatching towards us, so not knowing yet what the problem was with the helicopter we were obviously keen to get out of the thing as quickly as possible before it burst into flames. However, as soon as I opened the door I was able to use my engineering experience to detect the source of the clattering noise myself: I had left my seatbelt hanging out of the door.

'Stavros, you fucking idiot!' Barry shouted, and quick as a

flash he grabbed a screwdriver and started loosening one of the side panels on the helicopter. By the time the fire engines pulled up it looked as if that was the source of the problem, not me and my bloody seatbelt, and after about ten minutes of apologies and excuses we were cleared to go directly back to Charlwood, two or three miles away. As we sheepishly took off we heard one of the planes still in a holding pattern above us requesting urgent landing due to low fuel.

We lived every day to its fullest because we didn't know when it might end. On 28 July 1982 I thought that day had finally come. Barry was having a cracking year, finishing on the podium at six out of the seven races heading into our home Grand Prix at Silverstone and trailing Franco Uncini by twenty points with four races to go. It was a huge weekend for him in terms of the championship, but also because he had never actually won his home Grand Prix and he was desperate to do it before he retired.

After his fallout with Suzuki at the end of 1978, Barry had spent three seasons riding privateer Yamahas, playing second fiddle really to Kenny Roberts, who by now was the factory's golden boy, and rightly so, thanks to three consecutive World Championship titles. However, 1982 hadn't been a great season for Yamaha or Kenny and after he had pestered them for months they finally gave Barry a 'works' bike, meaning he had the top machinery available and full technical support from the factory and would soon be racing Kenny on virtually level terms at Silverstone.

It is hard to imagine nowadays, but on the Wednesday before the Grand Prix we went there for a practice day that was open to the public. There were 125s and 250s out there, with Barry lapping at record pace on the 500 until he came across a guy called Patrick Igoa, who had crashed his 250 on the exit of Abbey Corner. Barry didn't see him until the last second. When the crash happened I was back in the pits but it was one of those moments when you knew something serious had happened on the track. A deathly hush fell over the circuit, the scream of two-strokes giving way to late summer birdsong, and from about half a mile away we could see a thick plume of black smoke billowing up towards the sky.

Stephanie was in the paddock too, with Roman, her son from a previous marriage, and Barry's father Franco. Roman was convinced Barry had crashed but Steph told him not to be silly, that the smoke was from a stubble fire in a neighbouring field. Maybe it was the shock that sent her into denial but word soon came back that confirmed Roman's hunch. As soon as I found out it was Barry, I jumped on a scooter and went straight up there.

I arrived at what I can only describe as the scene of a plane crash, with Stephanie and Franco watching as Barry was carefully loaded into the ambulance. The bike had been a fireball and it was smashed to pieces all around us, with smouldering parts strewn all over the track. The rider wasn't in much better shape. The force of his legs hitting the handlebars as he flew over the top had smashed his knees and broken both of his shins. He had broken his wrist, his collarbone, some ribs . . . he had burns to his face and he just looked in such a bad way that I really don't think any of us imagined he could survive.

Barry and I had a pact that if either of us got into this kind of accident it was down to the other to try and find the best possible doctor in the area. I remember there was a row of phone boxes at Silverstone and journalist Nick Harris was in one filing his report of the crash back to *Motor Cycle News*, while I was in the next one and Franco was in the one next to me, frantically trying to sort out the best possible treatment for Barry. Over the years we had both got to know plenty of surgeons and I had a guy in Queen Mary's hospital in Sidcup called Rob Grey, so I phoned him up and told him the situation: that Barry was in a serious condition and I needed the best possible surgeon he could recommend. He came back with a name, Nigel Cobb, who by way of a miracle happened to be the orthopaedic surgeon at Northampton General, where Barry had been taken.

Nigel came down and had a look at Barry and although he couldn't do anything that night, the next day he conducted something like a nine and a half hour operation. Nigel said Barry's legs were so smashed up it was like a jigsaw trying to put everything back together, with the help of hundreds of screws, pins and plates. The job was made even harder by the fact that those legs had been badly broken before in a huge crash at Daytona, which had been caught on camera and shown on newsreels all around the world, helping to turn Barry into such a global household name. But this crash had been even bigger and the injuries were much worse.

Remarkably, a couple of weeks after the operation he seemed back to his old self, chatting up the nurses and cracking jokes for the television cameras, which he allowed into his ward. And just two months later he was back on a motorcycle, riding a Yamaha LC350 for a parade lap at Donington Park, where around 50,000 fans turned out to welcome him back. Even though his legs were still too weak to put down, he was lifted onto the bike with me sitting on the back acting as a stabiliser. I'd never felt so popular, with all those adoring girls waving their underwear at us. I waved back with a genuine smile on my face. I was literally back in Barry's slipstream and I couldn't have been happier to be there.

Barry returned to racing in 1983 and competed again in 1984, but the truth is he was never the same. How could you be after going through something like that? He was getting older, he had started a family and his will to win motorcycle races was finally being outdone by a will to survive and enjoy life, which he certainly did when he retired and moved to Australia in the late eighties.

By then we had been spending less time together anyway but I still missed him sorely, so I was glad that after a few years he started getting bored with the tranquillity of the Gold Coast and would come back to England for the opening of a crisp packet. As soon as he was home we would get back into our old double act, causing havoc wherever we went. One of his favourite annual jaunts was to the Gold Cup races at Oliver's Mount in Scarborough, where we had both won lots of races during our careers; we would get invites to do demo laps with other great former riders and friends like Phil Read, Roger Marshall and Mick Grant. It was always a fun weekend.

One year when Barry came back he borrowed a helicopter, an Agusta 109 worth about a million quid, from a friend of his. This chopper was the absolute bee's knees, with a retractable undercarriage, GPS and autopilot. No more following railway lines for us! It weighed something like three tonnes and cruised at 140 knots; it was a proper bit of kit. Perhaps the only problem with an Agusta 109 is that it's very thirsty and will only keep you in the air for a couple of hours before it needs refuelling. So the idea was to pick me up from my place, fly another 35 minutes or so up to an airport on the way, refuel and then make the short hop up to Scarborough.

By now I had a fixed-wing pilot's licence myself, so I knew all the correct aviation procedures, which include making contact with air traffic control from a minimum of six miles out of their airspace, telling them of your intention to enter with your height, your speed and everything else. But we got to within three miles of this particular airport and Barry was just flying along chatting away. Finally I interrupted him: 'Mate, don't we need to notify them that we're coming in?'

'Ah yeah, you're probably right,' he said, picking up the radio to air traffic control. 'This is Barry Sheene here in an Agusta 109. I wanna call in and pick up some fuel.'

It immediately became clear that Barry didn't have quite the same pull there as he had at Gatwick during the eighties. 'Helicopter Agusta 109 turn around one hundred and eighty degrees immediately,' came the response. 'We have several flights incoming and we cannot accommodate you at this time.'

I thought we were bang in trouble again. We turned around, hovered outside their airspace for a while and then tried again. This time I took over the radio in the more traditional fashion. 'This is N412 Echo Golf. We are an Agusta 109 at one thousand feet, inbound to you. We request fuel.'

'Yes, you can come in now,' the lady replied, 'but the pilot must report to the control tower immediately.' She then went on a little rant about us entering their airspace without permission, that we could have caused a major accident and so on.

We landed at the fuel bay and Barry said: 'Stavros, you fill it up. I'd better go up to the control tower and iron this thing out with the miserable old bat.' I reckoned we were probably going to get grounded and there was a chance Barry could even lose his licence for busting into her busy airspace.

By the time I'd put 450 litres of fuel in this helicopter he still wasn't back so I went up to the control tower to see what was going on. He was busting into her airspace alright! When I walked in I found him negotiating a 10 per cent discount on the fuel while signing his autograph on her left tit! You have to hand it to him. At least, she seemed keen to.

Eventually we left there and headed up to Scarborough. I asked Barry where we were staying. 'We've been booked into the Wrea Head Hotel,' he said. 'It's a huge place about three miles north of Scarborough with plenty of space to land, so we won't have a problem finding it.'

We hovered for a few minutes over Oliver's Mount to see the bikes going around but this thing was so thirsty on fuel the gauge was starting to go down already, so we pushed on north to try and find the Wrea Head. Twenty minutes later we were still looking for the damned place and I was midway through suggesting that we land anywhere and ask a local when Barry reckoned he'd spotted it. 'There it is over there! Big building, grass landing pad.' As we came down I could see the grass landing pad and assumed we were all good. Barry lowered the retractable landing gear and we hovered in. Out of the window all I could see was old people, some of them in wheelchairs, surrounding the lawn, which was absolutely pristine. I was convinced we were in the wrong place but as we touched down Barry insisted: 'Stavros, this must be it. You get out and double check!' So I jumped out of the helicopter and ran across the grass to ask one of the gentlemen watching on from his wheelchair. 'Is this the Wrea Head Hotel?' I shouted over the roar of the blades.

'No sir, this is the Miners' Union Retirement Home,' he shouted back, pointing at the helicopter. 'Is that Arthur?' He meant Arthur Scargill, the leader of the miners' union, who would apparently also drop by in a helicopter on the odd occasion, although presumably not into the middle of the bowling green.

I was just about to run back to tell Barry that we needed to get out of there when I was accosted by the groundsman of the home. We had landed our three-tonne Agusta 109 on their newly-laid bowling green and he was far from happy, so I legged it back to the chopper and climbed back in. 'So are we in the right place?' asked Barry.

'No, we bloody well are not!' I replied. 'Get this thing back up in the air as quick as you can!' We escaped and found the Wrea Head eventually, but it didn't take long for our escapade to get back to the newspapers.

The *Daily Mirror*

Barry Sheene landed on our bowling green

by Jeremy Armstrong

FORMER motorbike champ Barry Sheene landed his helicopter on a bowling green by mistake and got an earbashing from the groundsman.

Sheene was looking for a smart hotel when he spotted a big building from the air.

But as he touched down he found himself on the lawn of a miners' convalescent home and had the residents thinking that NUM President Arthur Scargill had dropped in.

Manager Mark Lomax said: 'We thought it was Arthur Scargill at first. He pops in now and again. The bowling green has just been relaid and it cost £17,500 so I was a bit worried. There are three small dents in it.'

Gardener Damien Barnett had just cut the new green and was having a rest when Sheene put his helicopter down on it.

Irate Damien said: 'He had a whole field to choose from and decided to land on the new green.

'I said to him "I've only just cut that" but he told me not to worry because the tyres were flat.

'It left three holes and I've had to fill them.'

Sheene's navigator Steve Parrish said: 'We were looking for a big building with a lawn out front and we just got muddled up.'

Sheene, due to take part in a parade of champions at a race day in Scarborough, joked: 'It's the first time I have been mistaken for Arthur Scargill and I hope it's the last.'

Thankfully, so far at least, that was also the last time either of us was mistaken for Arthur Scargill and eventually we were able to get up to Scarborough.

Mick Grant – three-times Motorcycle Grand Prix and seven-times TT winner

Stavros was up to his usual tricks whenever we met up in Scarborough and believe me I was more familiar with them than most, having been on the receiving end many times over the years. I remember being at an Auto 66 charity dinner in York, waiting for it all to start, chatting to the other guests and so on, and I saw these little yellow nibbles come out onto the table. I took one of these brightly coloured things, popped it into my mouth and immediately spat it out again because it tasted disgusting. To be honest I didn't think anything else about it until a couple of years later, when I read one of these tell-all interviews with Stavros in a magazine, where he revealed that he'd paid a waitress to put the urinal blocks on a plate and serve them to me! The bastard had done me and I didn't even know! I remember another time in Spain, when we were sleeping in adjacent bedrooms. I was laid in bed and about to fall asleep when I got showered in water. It was a typical shitty Spanish hotel with a bloody great hole in the wall, and somehow he had managed to tip a bucket of water through it – straight onto my head! The next night I'm wobbling about on a chair standing on top of a pile of books, trying to get him back. Grown men doing things like that . . . it's just not right, is it? Anyway, at Oliver's Mount he had this loud hailer with him and he kept using it to call a Dutch rider, Cees van Dongen, up to Race Control. Poor Cees would go up to Race Control, who had no idea what he was doing there and would tell him to piss off, only for Stavros to call for him to go back up again five minutes later. It was so bloody funny, but eventually Cees latched onto what was happening and later that afternoon, when we were all sitting around together having a cup of tea in this put-me-up awning, he tried to get his own back.

The Dutch lads had this strange little contraption they called a lung capacity tester. It looks like a little pipe with a windmill on the end of it, which spins around when you blow into it to give an indication of how strong your lungs are. Apparently, at one time they were used on miners to test the condition of their lungs. But this one was a joke one and unless you put it right into your mouth, covering this little hole with your tongue, it would blow soot all over your face.

So the guys started passing it around, all in on the prank, until it came to me. But Barry, being Barry, was so competitive that he reached over me and grabbed it first. 'Piss off Stavros,' he said, 'my lungs are way better than yours!' He always claimed that smoking had never affected him and that he could swim underwater further than the rest of us and everything else. So he grabbed hold of this thing, took a deep breath and gave it everything he had, sending the wheel spinning and a big black cloud of soot straight into his face. He was coughing and spluttering and looked like he'd just resurfaced after a long day at the coal face. We were all rolling around laughing while he jumped up and ran off to clean his face, past this long queue of autograph hunters, with all these dads telling their boys what a hero this man was supposed to be.

That memorable trip to Scarborough would prove to be one of our final escapades together. Two years later I received a phone call from Barry that I will never forget. 'I can't believe it, Stavros,' he said. 'I've got cancer.'

'Cancer of the what?' I replied, hoping it was one of his daft jokes.

'The oesophagus,' he said.

81

I instantly recalled another recent helicopter trip over to the North West 200 with Maggie Smart, Barry's sister, and another pilot friend of ours called Pete Barnes, who had actually instructed Barry through his conversion to the Agusta. 'Large' was a great character and an excellent pilot and as usual he was given his nickname by Barry, who picked up on one of his flying catchphrases: 'Give it large!' I hadn't been able to help but notice how much water Barry was drinking on that flight over, probably a litre an hour, which he claimed was due to the high temperatures in the air. I realised now that this phone call was no joke.

As strange as this sounds, I actually wasn't too concerned at first. There was a part of me thinking: 'Barry Sheene can't die from cancer. He's a two-time World Champion. He can beat anything!' But still my instinct was to try and fix it for him. It was what we had always done. I knew somebody who'd suffered from the same cancer and had had a successful operation to have a tube inserted, bypassing the oesophagus, so I put him in touch. But Barry didn't much fancy the idea of another operation.

He went down to a hospital in Brisbane and checked in with Stephanie. He had the usual forms to fill in and the nurse asked him if he was allergic to anything. 'Yeah, bloody cancer,' he said. This was three months into his diagnosis but he was still determined to make light of the situation. Then she asked him if he liked hospitals. 'No, I bloody hate them. I've spent enough time in these places.'

'Well, you're going to have to get used to being in one again!' she cheerfully replied. But with that Barry picked up his bag, grabbed Steph by the arm and walked out.

I spoke to him regularly over the phone after that and although he was acting the same I could tell there was something not right. The first time I saw him after he'd told me he had cancer was when he came back to Goodwood in the September and, despite the illness, won the Lennox Cup on a Manx Norton. He'd lost a stone and a half and joked that it was why the Norton was so fast, but there was no denying he looked ill and I could sense an element of trepidation in his voice. He went off to Mexico and saw different dieticians and had various alternative treatments, but none of it was working. Everybody who knew him and cared about him was telling him to have the operation but, typical of the stubborn old bastard, he wasn't having any of it.

That Christmas I had a call from an old friend called Julian Seddon, who back in the seventies was one of the main photographers' agents in London. His office on the King's Road was constantly full of all the top young models looking for work, flitting around the place like bees around a honey pot. Needless to say, Sheenie's Rolls-Royce would be parked outside on a pretty regular basis and they became close friends over the years.

Julian was in Australia, visiting Barry and Steph, and basically said: 'Look, Stavros, if you want to see Barry again you'd better get on the next flight.' I was shocked, but not as shocked as I would be when I landed in Brisbane a couple of days later. Before me was this tiny little person, drinking through a straw, quite literally a shadow of the indomitable champion I had once known.

Julian was out there with another friend of ours, Jeremy Paxton, who was Stephanie's brother-in-law. We stayed out there for a few weeks and met up with Mick Doohan, Daryl Beattie and a couple of Barry's other close friends over there, taking a trip together to Moreton Bay Island, just off the coast of southeastern Queensland. Mick is one of the hardest people I have ever met, a five-time 500cc World Champion who won all of his titles after breaking his leg, while Daryl was arguably equally talented but probably didn't have the same ruthless edge as Mick; the closest he came to the title was when he finished runner-up to Kevin Schwantz in 1993. One thing they had in common, as well as being Australian, was that they had both been helped out by Barry in their early days as racers, and had worked with him more latterly on Aussie television, and both of them had a huge amount of respect and admiration for the man they called 'Bazza'.

They are also both great company and Daryl, a notorious party animal, is always happy to be the butt of the jokes – especially when it comes to a rare injury he suffered at Le Mans in 1994, when he got one of his feet caught in the chain and lost all five toes. His toeless foot is a physical characteristic he's quite happy to take the piss out of and, in fact, his Twitter handle used to be @hangingfive, in reference to the surfing term 'Hanging Ten', when the surfer gets all his or her toes over the edge of the board.

We spent the whole night sitting under the stars, drinking beer, BBQing sausages and telling stories about Barry's life and how much he had helped us all over the years. Eventually we all fell asleep where we sat and woke up the next morning with terrible hangovers, bitten to death by the wretched mosquitoes.

I stayed on for a few days after that, but it was bloody hard eating normal meals with Steph and the family while Barry could only have liquids. I drove him a few times to the hospital, where he would have the fluids drained from his swollen stomach. By now he was around seven stone in weight; it was a dreadful sight. On the day that I was due to leave he made a Herculean effort to walk to the bottom of his large garden where he had built a new hangar to store a beautiful refurbished Agusta 109 helicopter, just like the one we had caused havoc with in the skies over the UK. It was a gorgeous thing with new avionics, paint job and interior and I just stood there looking at it, next to an owner who was far too sick to even contemplate flying it but was still immensely proud of himself for being able to buy it. I suppose it was symbolic of how far he had come in his life. It was sold many months later to a wealthy businessman from Brisbane and Steph wasn't surprised that on the day it was flown out of the Sheene estate there was heavy thunder and lightning all the way up the Gold Coast. Barry clearly wasn't impressed.

I spent the whole 24-hour journey back to the UK in tears and it was just a couple of weeks later, back home in Royston, when I got the call from Stephanie. I was expecting it, but it was still a huge shock and probably the first time in my whole life that I really let my emotions go. It made me realise that nobody is immortal, because in my eyes that's what Barry was. He was the one person who was always going to be there to look out for me and have fun with. He was Mr Fixit. If ever I needed anything I could always pick up the phone and say, 'What do you reckon to that?' or, 'I've only bloody gone and done this!' and he would help me out, without ever judging me. I had never experienced that closeness before. He was my best friend but he was also my father and my brother. Still, to this day, I can't believe that cancer got the better of him.

But I will always cherish that memorable last day we spent together on the Gold Coast and remember the words he uttered as we walked slowly back up from the hangar to their lovely manor house. Stopping to take a long look back at the Agusta, he said: 'Well Stavros, at least we will not die wondering.'

He didn't, and neither will I.

7

What a 6OCK!

Barry had a Rolls-Royce, so as soon as I became a factory motorcycle Grand Prix racer like him, I obviously decided I needed to have one too. I wasn't earning massive amounts of money and most of it was still going back into my racing, but I was able to pick up a six- or seven-year-old Shadow that I quickly realised I could sell on for a profit. An old Roller was the easiest car in the world to clock: you just undid four screws, took the glass off to remove the speedo, wound it back fifty thousand miles and then bodged it all back together again.

I got a pretty good return from the first two Rollers I had but I didn't get much change out of the third one. I took the speedo out and was just about to get to work when I saw a sticker, left by the previous owner, that read: 'Oh no, not again!' Some bastard had got to it before me! I was outraged that a Rolls-Royce owner would consider doing a thing like that.

There was undoubtedly something special about owning a Rolls-Royce, even a second-hand one. It was my way of saying to myself: 'Well done kid, you made it.' I guess I was fighting back against what people had said about me; proving them wrong, proving my father wrong. And there was no better opportunity to do that than when my old school, The Shrubbery, invited me back to present the sports day trophies in 1977. It was the first time in my life I had gone to school willingly, and I spent all morning polishing the Roller in preparation.

Of course, I hadn't really changed that much since I'd been expelled and I soon found that there's a lot you can get away with when driving a Rolls-Royce around a small village, such as cruising past the church on a Sunday morning and throwing flour bombs at people dressed in their Sunday best. They would be looking around for some hooligan in an Anglia or something, never suspecting the rich-looking gentleman in the flash motor.

With my penchant for trading cars it was rare for me to lose money on anything so nothing I drove was really an extravagance, no matter how fancy. I had the odd Jaguar, a Ford Mustang and a few Mercedes and for a while I was sponsored by Toyota, who loaned me a Supra – their equivalent of the 3.0 litre Ford Capri – but it wasn't until 1984, when I got a deal on a Mercedes through Barry, that I actually bought anything new. The flash cars were fun while they lasted but I always found that there's actually a lot more excitement to be had from driving something daft.

Frankie Parrish

On my twenty-first birthday my dad parked his hearse, complete with fake arm sticking out of the side of a coffin, outside my birthday party at Grantchester Hall in Cambridge. My friends, some of whom had travelled all the way down from Newcastle University, thought they had the wrong venue and started to turn back. As dad travelled a lot for work, summer holiday heaven for us was two weeks on the coast in Norfolk. We had a lot of gear to take: jet-ski, quad bike, bicycles, etc., but instead of using a trailer dad bought a retired ambulance at auction. Not only could he fit all the gear in the back, but if the traffic was bad he could stick on the siren and whizz up the hard shoulder. But by far the most embarrassing was the bright yellow, three-wheeled van he had made to look identical to the one in *Only Fools and Horses*. He would come skidding into the playground to drop me off at school, almost tipping the van onto its side, and I'd have to clamber past the blow-up sex doll to get my book bag.

I have taken great pleasure from embarrassing my children over the years, like when I set myself up as the first ever UK distributor for battery-operated fart machines, an ingenious little invention that I had discovered on a trip to the USA. I used to sell them via mail order through magazines like *Viz*, and the kids earned their pocket money putting batteries in and testing each one to make sure it worked before packaging them all up and posting them off. It made us a few quid but by far the best thing about the whole operation was the company name. Hearing Frankie reluctantly answering the telephone with 'Hello, Parrish Poo Poos!' kept me entertained for years.

But there was nothing quite as much fun as dropping her off at school in that wonderful 'Trotters Independent Trading' van, which I came across by sheer chance when I was on my way back from a race meeting at Oulton Park. I had ended up driving through some downtrodden suburb of Birmingham after being diverted off the M6 when I saw it sitting on a driveway with a 'For Sale' sign in the window. It was a bright blue three-wheeled van that in every other way was identical to the one driven by my hero Derek Trotter and I immediately thought: 'I've got to get myself one of those!' So I parked up the Merc and knocked on the front door of the house.

A chap answered and it immediately became clear that this car was his pride and joy. He insisted that if he was to sell it to me I must be sure to take the Reliant owners' club book with me and send off all the forms to become a member. 'Of course I will,' I lied, stifling a laugh and agreeing to come back the following day to collect the van. The next morning I took my good friend John Brown, a big, strong ginger lad with freckles and a heart of gold, with me back up to Birmingham with a trailer. Naturally, it hadn't occurred to us that you can't load a three-wheeled vehicle up a two-ramp trailer, so after a lot of laughing and some improvisation with a scaffold plank that we found lying around on the estate we eventually got her loaded up.

I spent a fortune on that van, getting it repainted and sign-written to look just like the one Del Boy drove on the television, complete with the blow-up doll in the back window. I even had the engine fitted with diesel injection and altered the timing so that it backfired, sending out plumes of black smoke. That car was the start of a bit of an addiction to unusual vehicles and once I realised how much fun there was to be had with them, I started stretching the idea a little further.

I bought the ambulance from a private hospital, initially so I could take the family Christmas shopping in London although, as Frankie said, it proved even more handy for shooting down to Great Yarmouth through the busy Bank Holiday traffic on the M11. I then went to a military auction and bought an armoured car, which I eventually sold on to Ralph Bryans, a brilliant little rider who remains Ireland's only Grand Prix World Champion, having won the 50cc title in 1965. Ralph was from Belfast but had moved to Glasgow and was fed up with getting his car kicked in at Glasgow Rangers football matches, although I have no idea how he managed to drive the bloody thing because he was barely tall enough to see through the little slit at the front.

The first hearse I bought was from an undertaker's in Bourne, Lincolnshire. Again, how I kept a straight face about it I've no idea, but I phoned up and enquired about the vehicle. The bloke said, 'You *are* in the business, aren't you?' so I spun him a story that I worked for the local undertaker in Royston and we were looking for a secondary vehicle in case ours broke down. I even put a black suit on to go up there, trying to look as sombre as possible, and bought it for £1,500. It was an Austin Princess and it stank of piss and old people but it had a big engine in it and I was giggling all the way home at the look on people's faces as I blasted past them at 100mph down the outside lane of the A1. I drove the bloody thing home so hard the exhaust fumes melted the plastic on the fog lights! It made me laugh because the car had probably never been over fifty before.

I bought a coffin and a plastic arm for extra effect and Terry Rymer, who rode for my team at the time, got me a police siren for it. I don't know where he got it from or even why, but we caused so much confusion while tearing around in a hearse going 'NEE-NAW!', with the lights flashing on the top. We actually caused an accident in Royston one day when I came flying out of the town centre and overtook this poor bloke, who just stared at us like, 'What the . . .. ?' and drove straight into the back of another car. On another occasion I had four friends in the thing, driving to Watford, when we got stuck in a traffic jam. After a while I went 'Sod this', and drove all the way down the outside of the queue, only to cut back in just two cars behind another hearse. It wasn't a traffic jam at all but an actual funeral cortège!

One morning I went over to Cambridge Crematorium with a coffin in the back. A bloke came out with a clipboard and said: 'Good morning. I'm sorry, but we're not even lit yet.' I said, 'Oh bollocks, we'll go somewhere else then!' and sped off, skidding the hearse all the way up the gravel drive back to the main road.

In the end the hearse got rusty and conked out but by then it had given me so much pleasure that I told an old sponsor of mine, Bill Fry, who was an undertaker, that as soon as he got a new one I would have his old one. So the second hearse I bought was a Daimler from Bill, which ironically almost proved to be the end of me and my girlfriend Michelle, when for some reason I decided to drive it down to Barnstaple in Devon. Just as we arrived it started pissing down with rain and all the windows steamed up, so I asked Michelle to get in the back and wipe them down. Just as she was doing that we went down a hill and the brakes failed. I pumped them and pumped them but only one wheel was locking on and we were screeching and skidding down this hill. Some poor bloke stepped out onto the zebra crossing and I almost ran over his toes as we went flying through, with the horn blaring and Michelle rolling around in the back. I bet he still wonders what on earth was going on there.

It occurred to me that having a real-life prop in the back was a brilliant idea, so I managed to persuade my good mate John Brown to let me wrap him in cling film and then get in the hearse. With nothing on but a pair of skin-coloured underpants he rolled around in the back scaring the life out of people as I smoked the tyres around roundabouts and all sorts.

Once we were bored of the hearse, Brownie and I decided to go halves on a fire engine, a 1960s Karrier that we bought from Old Warden Aerodrome in Bedfordshire. After picking it up, complete with six firemen's suits, axes and all the other accessories, we stopped at the first place we thought we could cause trouble, which happened to be an Indian restaurant on the roundabout near Royston. We hurtled in through the restaurant and into the kitchen with the hosepipe shouting: 'FIRE! FIRE!' After clearing the whole place, we then just retreated to the truck pissing ourselves laughing and drove off before they called the police!

We put that truck to wonderful use, perhaps most constructively at a Genesis concert at Knebworth in 1992. We couldn't get tickets so we just turned up with four other mates, all dressed up in the firemen's uniforms. We didn't even need to speak to anybody; they just moved the barriers out of the way and beckoned us through, directing us right down to a spot next to St John Ambulance in front of the stage. We were so convincing we even put a collection bucket out and came home with some beer money for the pub that evening!

We also used the fire engine in lieu of an invite at the fiftieth birthday party of a gentleman called Hugh Chamberlain, who was the owner of a prolific World Endurance team that used to run the Jaguar effort at Le Mans. Hugh was a jolly, well-spoken chap, a people person rather than a businessman, and his party, which was sure to be a grand affair, was to be held in a marquee in the beautiful gardens of his house, a lovely eighteenth-century building with a thatched roof in Buntingford. Brownie and I were a bit put out not to be invited, but we knew some of the people who were, including Hugh's loyal and talented chief engineer Derek Kemp, who was a mate of ours.

We gave Derek a smoke bomb to let off at exactly 8.30 p.m. and then waited around the corner, again dressed up in the firemen's uniforms that came with the truck. At exactly 8.35 p.m. we came charging through the gates, pulled up right next to the marquee and jumped out. In a carefully rehearsed manoeuvre Brownie unravelled the hoses, I undid the taps and this time we let them rip. Even though it was an old fire engine it had a lot of pressure and it took two of us to hold the four-inch-wide hose steady, with Brownie at the front. All of the guests were dressed up in black tie and evening gowns and they all started running from the marquee back towards the house.

It was like something from the television show *It's a Knock-out* as these poor buggers ran for cover, their legs getting blasted out from under them in a barrage of water that sent them spinning across the wet grass. Every time one of them made a break for safety, Brownie took them out like a sniper. He must have claimed ten or more victims by the time Hugh realised what was going on and ran to the pumps to turn them off. We were told in no uncertain terms where to go and it took Hugh a while to see the funny side, but I interviewed him at an event at Silverstone a few years later and we had a good laugh. It seems none of his guests forgot that night.

As well as the standard uniforms, the fire engine came with this bright silver asbestos outfit, complete with gas mask, that looked like a space suit. So when I wore it to a folk music festival at Wimpole Park, which we also gained free access to in the fire engine, the bloke in charge assumed I was responsible for the fireworks. He kept coming up to me saying: 'Are you ready yet?' So I kept replying: 'No, no, just give us another ten minutes.' The band were due to stop playing at 9.30 p.m. but he kept them going for another hour while he kept coming back to me to ask if we were ready. Of course, I had absolutely nothing to do with the fireworks but by the time they realised this half the fuses had burned out and the whole display was ruined.

Mucking around in a fire engine is not something you would get away with nowadays and even though these were more in-nocent times I suppose it should come as no surprise to you by now that I became quite familiar with the local constabulary in the Royston area. They hadn't liked it when I purchased an American police bike like the one from the TV show *CHiPS*, and they would regularly stop me even driving my normal cars, which always had daft number plates like my all-time favourite PEN15, which I eventually sold, and 6OCK, which I still have to this day. Originally I got them because my wife kept driving my nice Mercedes, so I put them on to deter her. Suffice to say, PEN15 would get pulled quite regularly because they claimed the letters and numbers were too close together, but I always assured them it was just because it was a cold day. They never swallowed it.

One officer in particular, who we will call Sergeant Atkins, was always giving me and Brownie grief for one thing or another, so in the end we decided to properly stitch him up. Unlike me, Brownie was actually a genuine second-hand car dealer by trade so he knew just what to do. We found out his address and bought six old bangers with no MOTs or logbooks from a mate's scrapyard. Then we sent off to the DVLA for new logbooks, all in Sergeant Atkins' name, and on the night before we reckoned they were due to be delivered to his house we went into action.

We gathered a bunch of mates together and set off in the cars, travelling from my workshops at the farm down to Letchworth. These things all had bald tyres and hardly any lights on them and we had to jumpstart half of them to get them going. We took the back roads down via Ashwell, through Hinksworth, and came up to a T-junction where we would be turning left towards Letchworth. There was a lady in a car already at the junction, waiting to turn right, when Brownie pulled up alongside her in the lead car. I was in the third car back so I thought it would be great fun to smash into the guy in front, who then smashed into Brownie. The guys behind all joined in and before you knew it we had a six-car pile-up! The poor lady got out of her car with a pen and paper, ready to act as a witness, when we all just screeched off, leaving bits of bumpers and lights behind on the road and waving out of our windows, going: 'Don't worry love!'

Once we got to Letchworth we parked every car on double yellow lines in different places around the town, dropped every set of keys down a drain and went home. On the first day the cars had parking tickets on them. On the second day they were displaying 'POLICE AWARE' stickers. And on the third day, Sergeant Atkins found out that he owned the bloody lot! Strangely enough, we never saw much of him after that, although I did hear that somebody had paid the scrapyard a visit, asking for information on the purchaser of the vehicles. It's certainly good to have friends in the right places!

8

You'd better watch out

It wasn't just Sergeant Atkins who had a bone to pick with me and before long my antics would catch up with me in quite spectacular fashion; on national television, no less. It all started with the landlord of the Waggon and Horses in Steeple Morden, Steve Roberts, who was pissed off because I'd pulled up in the fire engine one sunny evening and soaked the place with the hose. I guess I underestimated the power of the water, which smashed everything in its path to bits and flooded the pub. In the end they had to shut down for a couple of days while they dried the place out, so I can see why he was annoyed.

Brownie also owed me for a couple of pranks I'd played on him so between them they got together and hatched a plan to get me back, with the help of famous TV wind-up merchant Jeremy Beadle. They wrote a letter to London Weekend Television explaining that there was some twat in the village making everybody's life a misery, who they reckoned would be the perfect subject for an episode of *Beadle's About*. LWT got straight back and said they were interested, so Brownie put them in touch with Yamaha and Loctite, who were my main sponsors at the time, to organise a plausible sting.

A week before the 'get', I received a message from Ray Ross and Andy Smith at Yamaha saying that I needed to come into

London for a ten o'clock meeting on the following Tuesday. At the same time I had a call from Loctite, saying they had a trade journalist from 'Glue International' or some other such completely fabricated magazine, who wanted to come down to my workshops and do a feature. The lady came and I took her around, talking about the bikes and explaining how we worked on them and showing her where we paint the fairings and everything else. She seemed pretty interested but in reality, of course, she was casing the joint for LWT.

Without suspecting a thing, I jumped in my van at seven o'clock on the Tuesday morning and headed down to London for my meeting with Yamaha. Normally, whenever I went down to Yamaha around that time it would always be followed by lunch and maybe a glass of wine, but on this occasion we finished up at around midday and the guys were like: 'Okay Steve, thanks a lot, seeya!' It struck me as a little odd but I jumped back in the van, headed home and picked up some doughnuts from Days bakery at Ashwell. That's why, if you ever get to see the clip, you'll see I'm licking my lips and scoffing a doughnut when I arrive back at the farm.

You'll also see that I was greeted on the driveway by a police officer, who asked me for my driving licence. Considering my form there were any number of matters that this could have been related to so my mind immediately started whirring, but clearly I couldn't help but notice that my land was swarming with US Army vehicles and personnel. The policeman told me that the farm had been sealed off for two days for a NATO operation and I have to say it looked convincing. There were barricades everywhere, soldiers in full combat gear running about all over the place with guns, helicopters overhead and a bloody great tank racing up and down my fields. The next thing, there was an almighty 'BOOM' and the air was filled with smoke as one of these huge cannons let off a round.

The policeman introduced me to a senior-looking soldier called Colonel Fudpucker – at least that's what it said on the name tag between the medals on his uniform – who asked what I was doing 'in his area'. I said: 'Well, I drove down the lane because I live here.' I was smiling because I reckoned it had to be a wind-up, but I just couldn't be sure. And besides, who did I know who could afford a stunt like this? 'What we've got here is a temporarily restricted zone for this operation, you shouldn't be here,' said Colonel Fudpucker, pulling out a map. 'I don't know what you're doing here. But the co-ordinates for where we're supposed to be is Gatley End Farm, 52.0661 degrees north, 0.1251 degrees west.' I jumped in to inform him that this was not Gatley End Farm but Church Farm and with that he was straight on the radio: 'Alpha Bravo Zero One, we are at the wrong location – cease fire!'

But it was too late. A missile landed in my garden and blew a massive hole in the ground, sending a thick cloud of black smoke and debris into the air. That was followed by another, and another, and another, getting closer and closer to the workshops where my bikes and all the equipment were. At the back of my mind I was still convinced it had to be a wind-up but the whole thing was so bloody realistic I started to get worried. 'Before you blow it up can I get my truck and bikes out?' I asked one of the more senior-looking officers, who had just arrived on the scene in a military sidecar.

The sheer size of the explosions was nothing if not convincing and to top it off there were bits of bike fairings and other bits and pieces amid all the debris flittering down through the sky. I thought: 'They really are blowing up my fucking workshops!' I started swearing a bit but then I noticed they all had guns so I watched my mouth in case they shot me. My brain was utterly fried so it took me a few moments to realise what was happening when the bloke stuck a microphone under my nose and then revealed himself as one of the most famous faces on television at the time. I had been well and truly 'Beadled'. Standing beside him in full combat gear was that total bastard Brownie.

To be fair it was a good wind-up and it turned out to be one of the largest *Beadle's About* shows LWT ever did, with a huge budget. But my motto has always been 'Don't get mad, get even', and as far as I am concerned it doesn't matter how long that takes. I don't care who started it, if you play a prank on me you're getting done back, and that was exactly what would happen to every member of the mob that stitched me up that day – starting with Geoff Bennett, the managing director of Loctite.

Geoff was a tall, smart, well-dressed guy who worked hard and partied harder and his company car was a Porsche, which he used to take to a place near Loctite's base in Welwyn Garden City to be serviced by a company called Wellspray, who happened to be friends of mine. He took his car in for a full valet and service one day, so the guys called me up and said: 'Stavros, we've got Geoff Bennett's car here.' I got some stuff together, went down there and while the guys worked on the service I spent about five hours re-plumbing his windscreen washers through the bulkhead of the car, with extra pipes that came up through the steering column, held in place with tie wraps. I put some carburettor main jets in the pipes and directed them so that when he went to spray his windscreen the water would squirt straight between his legs.

Luckily for the benefit of the finer details of this story, Geoff had a passenger with him on his first ride in his freshly-serviced Porsche – Loctite's sales director Phil Corke, who would later fill me in on exactly what happened. Geoff and Phil had had a big argument about an irate customer up in Wolverhampton; Geoff was furious and basically told Phil that since he couldn't sort this complaint out himself, they were going to have to head up there together and smooth things over.

It was winter, so Geoff was wearing a fairly thick woollen suit, and as they set off for Wolverhampton he was still in a foul mood, moaning about the bad weather, the traffic and everything else. Not long into their journey a lorry came past and covered them with filthy spray, so Geoff naturally went for the windscreen washers. 'Zzzzz, zzzzz.' He tried a couple of times, but of course nothing happened. 'Zzzzz, zzzzzzzzzzzz.' Still nothing . . . or so he thought, because his trousers were so thick the water hadn't actually soaked through yet. 'Those wankers at Wellspray!' he was moaning. 'I took it in for a full service and they haven't even filled the fucking windscreen washers!'

At this point Phil spotted what was going on and, knowing me, realised who was responsible. 'This happened to my car,' he offered Geoff. 'There's probably a blockage or something. Just hold the thing on.' So Geoff gave it a big handful, 'Zzzzzzzzzzzzzzzz!' and completely soaked his bollocks! By the time they got to Wolverhampton he was still drenched, so he sent Phil in on his own to deal with this unhappy customer while he sat outside and stewed his nuts in a puddle of water and washer fluid. Phil went in and managed to smooth things over with the customer but on his way back out he was handed a note by the receptionist. It simply read: 'Get the fucking train home, I've gone.'

To hear the juicy details of a successful outcome like that was a bonus, because often I don't have that pleasure. To me the satisfaction usually lies in knowing I have done somebody, rather than getting to witness it first-hand. Rarely, however, do I have to wait as long to find out if a prank has come off than when I hit Brownie in one of a long series of jokes that we played on each other in the years after the *Beadle's About* thing. Neither of us will ever be prepared to call a truce, so the pranks go back and forth, back and forth. And this particular opportunity rather dropped into my lap when I myself was the victim of a wind-up from my neighbour and great friend Dave Morris.

Since we met through our mutual love of flying some twenty years ago, Dave has become one of my best mates and is now my next-door neighbour, ever since I bought my house on his land at Top Farm, right next to the grass landing strip that runs behind his huge hangar. I call it the Top Farm Triangle, because so many strange things seem to happen up there. Every day somebody has fallen off their horse, a plane has tipped over or Dave has bought a new weird and wonderful animal to keep in the pen. Even his wife and his daughter once had a head-on crash on the driveway. I love all that chaos and Dave is a great laugh to be around so we make ideal neighbours.

This particular incident happened in November 2009, when Michelle and I arrived home from the final round of the MotoGP season at Valencia to find a handwritten note on the door of the spare room that said 'The Horny Room'. We pushed the door open and there resting between the pillows of the bed was a stag's head, complete with a pair of giant sunglasses and a fag dangling from its mouth, looking rather cool and relaxed between our Egyptian cotton sheets. I won't lie, I have seen a number of strange things in my bed, but this one was something of a shock.

I had a pretty good idea how it got there, since Dave also happens to be a qualified butcher. I should point out at this juncture, to any animal lovers reading this, that the stag had been hit by a lorry on the main road outside the farm gates. Naturally, when Dave came across it, he chainsawed the head off and broke into my house. It's what any right-minded individual would have done.

Likewise, on encountering this amusing, if rather inconvenient, scene in my spare bedroom, my devious mind also went into overdrive and I decided that the severed noggin of this poor beast could serve a further purpose. It was about eleven o'clock at night but I said to Michelle: 'Come on, we need to get Brownie with this.'

With Rudolph's head wrapped up in a bin liner, we set off on our mission to Blunham, where Brownie was in the process of restoring a very old but beautiful water mill and its house and grounds. He'd just had some super-duper electric gates fitted at the entrance to the long impressive drive, upon which – under the cover of darkness and wearing balaclavas – we impaled the stag's head using wire coat hangers.

The next morning, I fully expected to get a phone call or a visit from Brownie but it was all strangely quiet until Boxing Day that year, when we attended our annual karting event, where we would see who could drive the fastest with the most mulled wine in them at Brownie's private track. Conversation eventually moved on to the dead stag, with Dave still highly amused about his successful 'head in the bed' prank on me. As Dave regaled everybody with this tale, a sudden look came over Brownie's face.

It turned out that unbeknownst to us Brownie had been on holiday when we stuck the head on his gate and he'd left the builders to look after the house. They'd been having some problems with travellers trying to set up a site on the land and before he'd gone away Brownie had had quite a serious run-in with them, which ended up with two of these blokes getting thrown into the river. The builders put two and two together and called Brownie in Mallorca: 'John, we've got a problem. We daren't go onto the site because there's a Gypsy death threat on the gate.'

With the builders on strike, poor Brownie and Sue cut their

holiday short and flew straight back to deal with the matter, with Sue booking herself and their daughter Georgie into a nearby hotel because she refused to go near the house. She stayed there for two weeks, while Brownie and their son Charlie, who was around fifteen at the time, kept lookout at the house. Brownie would use searchlights and binoculars at night to survey the ground for intruders and every morning he would bundle Charlie into the back seat of the car and get him to lie down all the way to school in case they got shot at! Eventually, when they felt enough time had passed, Sue and Georgie returned home and life got back to normal.

You can imagine how furious he was now, having finally realised who was responsible. Not only had he cut short his holiday and been forced to pay the builders for wasted time, he'd even reported the whole story to the police and his family were pretty traumatised. That wasn't my intention, of course, but I had no idea he'd had this run-in with the travellers! Anyway, I knew JB only too well, so I knew that from that moment on he would already be planning his revenge, which finally came around a year later, when I least expected it and had stupidly let my guard down.

By this time Sue was finally speaking to me again and they had invited us round to the now completely and beautifully refurbished mill house for supper, along with another couple called Malcolm and Stephanie Gammons, who were mutual friends of ours. We had been given a tour of the mill and had already sunk a few glasses of wine when we were invited to take our place at the dining table. Unusually for such an informal occasion, the table was set with place names – a glaring clue to what might be to come, which I foolishly missed. I was sitting opposite Malcolm, whom I had met before through racing, and we had a delightful evening – eating, drinking, telling stories, like you do. After a lovely supper the coffee and brandy came out and I was just about to take my first sip of coffee when, suddenly, all hell broke loose.

I don't know how long Brownie had spent setting this up but he'd screwed the table to the floor and then got a large CO_2 gas bottle with a fast release tap and some Goodridge braided steel piping and fixed it all to the underside of the table, with the jet firing straight at my bollocks. Brownie claims that he thought he'd released most of the pressure, with the idea of giving me a relatively gentle, if surprising, blast in the balls. However, when he actually pulled the pin there was still about 1000psi in this bloody thing and the sheer force of it blasted me backwards off my chair, across the kitchen floor and slammed me against the opposite wall! It was so sudden and so unexpected. I didn't have a clue to what was happening, while poor unsuspecting Malcolm almost had a heart attack. The scene was like something from *The Exorcist*; me lying slumped against the wall, covered in coffee!

Things calmed down a little after that one, but along with Brownie, Dave and a couple of other friends we still like to entertain ourselves by playing the odd, relatively harmless trick – such as bricking up each other's houses or fly-tipping in the gardens. One weekend when I was away at the racing I was having some builders in to do some work on the house and when we came back there was a full-on brass dancing pole erected in the middle of my living room. When the kids came around and asked what it was doing there I had to convince them that the builders had moved the water tank upstairs and the pole was propping up the living room ceiling.

You would never quite know exactly who was responsible, so you would just pass the 'favour' on in the knowledge that, eventually, it would come back to you. One such occasion was when another close neighbour of mine, Jimmy Carter – known as the 'Pie Man' for obvious reasons – asked to borrow my big four-wheel-drive Mercedes to go to Calais and stock up on booze. He brought it back all clean, full of fuel, and everything seemed fine until a week or so later I started to notice this funny smell. Over the next few days it got worse and worse until I virtually pulled the car apart and found this round of stinky French cheese, which Jimmy had purposely hidden under the spare wheel. My opportunity to get him back arose when he went on holiday and foolishly gave Dave Morris his house keys so that he could mow his lawn while he was away. As soon as Jimmy was gone, we embarked on a project we called 'Operation Alpaca'.

We loaded Dave's trailer up with one of the alpacas from his farm and then swung by a mate's turkey farm to pick up a couple of birds. We then went round to Jimmy's with a camcorder and filmed a spoof episode of *Through the Keyhole*, with the bloody alpaca and the turkeys all running riot around the house. Jimmy was a massive, massive Chelsea fan so we put the alpaca in an Arsenal scarf for extra effect. We cleaned the house up afterwards so that he didn't suspect a thing and that Friday evening when he got back we all met for a pint down at Michelle's old pub, the Queen Adelaide in Croydon, where we played the DVD on the big screen.

Some years ago I had been telling Geoff Bennett about a similar escapade, while we were on a shooting excursion with some other Loctite top brass in Cheltenham, and he asked me if I could stitch up Phil Corke for him. I knew Phil loved a practical joke, unless it was on him. 'No problem,' I said, 'I can do it right now.' As usual, I had a box of tricks on hand in the boot of my car, including some stage maroons, which are small explosives that they use in theatres for when the genie pops out of the lamp or whatever. They look almost like a loo roll with two leads coming out, which detonate the gunpowder as soon as they come into contact with an electrical current.

I had already run a few experiments with these things on the team's works pickup truck, which was a shitty old brown Austin Marina. My ingenious idea was to connect the leads to the brake lights and then position the stage maroon for maximum surprise effect, such as inside a small bag of flour tucked behind the sun visor. The poor unsuspecting guinea-pig for my first attempt was my mechanic Dave 'Mushroom' Johnson (so called because he was always kept in the dark and we fed him on bullshit). Dave jumped into the truck to go and buy another pie and just as he drove out of the yard he touched the brakes and got the fright of his life when the whole thing blew up in his face! I couldn't believe how well it had worked and started to invent different uses for these ingenious theatrical props. Anyway, while everybody was busy having a drink and a chat, I nipped outside to Phil's brand-new company car, a top-of-the-range 3 Series BMW, and wired a stage maroon up to the brake lights, ran the wires under the car and planted it under the bonnet.

We were due to have dinner at this place but as luck would have it Phil had to leave early, so he said his goodbyes and went out to his car. Everybody else ran to the window to watch as he got in and set off down to the end of the lane, where there was a cattle grid. Now to be honest, this particular stage maroon was a bit bigger than it needed to be for the job, and instead of just making a bang and giving poor Phil a shock, the moment he touched the brakes the thing exploded so hard it blew the bonnet clean off! Of course, Phil absolutely shat his pants; he didn't know what had happened to his beautiful new car.

We were all crying with laughter and of course Loctite weren't bothered – business was flying and they had plenty of money to pay for the repair. Meanwhile, I was coming up with even better, more expensive ways for them to blow their cash.

9

Sticking together

'You have to pay. You have to pay, now.' The Spanish coppers weren't having any of my excuses and now Brownie and I
found ourselves at a petrol station on the outskirts of Barcelona
having to cough up a hundred euros that these bastards were
sure to stick straight in the back pockets of their ridiculously
tight motorcycling pants. In fairness, it was quite remarkable
that we hadn't been pulled up sooner, having driven Brownie's
classic Ford Mustang all the way through France at well over
100mph for most of the journey.

We were on our way to Mallorca, where we both had an
apartment, and had been escorted off the motorway by these
two tight-trousered tight-fists just a few miles from the port
and taken to the nearest cashpoint. There was no way out of
it, but while they followed Brownie to the machine I quickly
grabbed a tube of Loctite from my bag and covered the seats
and handlebars of their motorcycles with the stuff. Brownie
came back out, hopped into the car and said: 'They're actually
not bad blokes you know. They're going to show us the quick
way back to the motorway.'

'No, they're bloody well not!' I replied, and as soon as they
pulled out onto the road, we pissed off as fast as we could go in
the opposite direction.

I have always been anti-authoritarian ever since those days back in Steeple Morden when the bobbies would chase Geoff Sturgess and me home from the garage with our pockets full of sweets and over the years I have exacted swift revenge on coppers all over the world, like in the Czech Republic once, when I got pulled over outside a restaurant near the circuit in Most. They were being typically awkward, demanding my passport and driving licence and generally messing me about for half an hour, before eventually letting me go without so much as a fine. As I walked back to my car I noticed they'd left their keys on their bonnet so I just took my chance and swiped them into my pocket. All the team were in the restaurant and we spent the most enjoyable half an hour ever watching them blaming each other and searching for their keys before eventually another car came to pick them up!

I constantly entertained myself with Loctite, gluing people's drinks down and sticking stuff together. It was a match made in heaven, and you could say that on the track the bond was just as strong. After six years of sponsoring me as a rider, I pulled a pretty good move to make sure they continued to stick by me when I finally decided to hang up my leathers in 1987, by making Geoff Bennett the godfather to my newly-born daughter Frankie. That was probably the most sensible bit of parenting I have ever done. The daftest, in case you're wondering, was when I faked Frankie's date of birth on her enrolment forms and despite her mother's protests sent her off to school a year early just to get her out from under our feet. Her birthday is in September, and it was a damn sight cheaper than another year of childcare.

They eventually found out, of course, and poor Frankie had to resit reception, with all her classmates assuming she was staying down because she had learning difficulties. Meanwhile I got away with it, blaming my own learning difficulties when filling out the form. Otherwise, I was taking my responsibilities as a father quite seriously and it felt like the right time to take a step back from the inherent dangers of racing motorcycles. Besides, at the age of 33, I knew I wasn't getting any faster and I had it at the back of my mind from the start of 1986 that it would be my final season as a rider. Meanwhile, I also knew Loctite were keen to maintain a two-rider team for 1987, so the logical step was for me to keep the whole thing rolling and continue to spend their money for them in the guise of team manager.

It was a natural transition for me because I had spent my whole racing career looking after myself. Right from those early club racing days, with my Pourus Racing drinking pals, I had looked after my own bikes at my workshop, employed my own mechanics, organised my own sponsorship and arranged all the logistics of getting myself on the grid both at home and abroad. I owned the trucks, I owned the caravans, I paid the mechanics' wages. Even during that one season as a factory rider with the Texaco Heron Suzuki team in 1977, Suzuki GB just gave us the bikes: even though they would have a support truck at the races we always took them back to our own workshops at the end of the weekend. It was unusual but it was how Barry had always done it. The Japanese at Suzuki weren't keen on the idea of having their precious factory bikes anywhere but at their own workshops and it was actually one of the reasons why Barry split with them at the end of 1979 and went to Yamaha.

In 1980 I was sponsored by Bill Fry, a generous and rotund little fellow who was much more fun than I expected an undertaker would be. He bought me a 500cc Suzuki and a TZ750 Yamaha, with some sponsorship from Shell and Dunlop. It was a transitional year, and then in 1981 Barry worked his magic again and convinced Robert Jackson from Mitsui Yamaha that they needed Steve Parrish. I couldn't have got in at a better time with Yamaha, who had LC350s flying out of the window and more cash and toys than they knew what to do with. The amount of gear you could blag off them was ridiculous – I'd go down to their warehouse in Chessington in my big truck, back it up and say, 'We need another minibike and a quad bike', and they'd just load them up. They had a system, a bit like a clocking-in machine, where they checked off what you'd taken on a card. But, of course, anybody with a Yamaha contract was using each other's cards and driving away with van loads of gear in somebody else's name.

Even though I was no longer a full-time World Championship rider, from 1981 to 1986 I did selected Grands Prix, British Championship races and road races like the TT, the NW200 and the Macau Grand Prix with some decent results, including a bunch of wins at Scarborough, a podium at the French Grand Prix at Nogaro and a European Championship win at Donington Park. When you add in other international events like the Transatlantic Match Races, I was competing in close to thirty events per season and obviously all of that took a lot of logistical preparation.

In footballing terms I was a player-manager years before Kenny Dalglish made the job famous. I learned how to run a business, which in racing meant putting yourself out there, finding the sponsors, coming back with the money and budgeting it accordingly. I knew inside out what it took to run a successful operation and I knew that, first and foremost, the most important thing to have was good bikes, which we had thanks to the continued support of Yamaha. I also knew I had some cracking good mechanics, led by Adrian Gorst, a straight-talking Kiwi who worked hard and expected everybody else to do the same, so I set about the task of getting the riders to match. And I knew exactly where to start.

Kenny Irons was a fresh-faced, happy-go-lucky young kid who sprang to my attention when I raced against him at the start of my final season in 1986. Along with Ray Swann and Kev Wrettom, Kenny was one of a trio of talented, streetwise youngsters known throughout the paddock as the 'Luton Mafia', who had arrived with backing from some small local sponsors in Luton. Kenny had a Suzuki and an FZ750 Yamaha, which he was racing in the Superstock category, so I threw him some extra spares, a bit of cash and a few tubes of glue in exchange for painting his Yamaha in our Loctite colours. Technically he was still doing his own thing, but I wanted to make sure it was our team that was seen to win that title and, since I knew I wasn't going to do it myself, I backed Kenny.

I even gave him my own bike to ride at a couple of meetings, at Oulton and Scarborough, when he had problems with his, and helped enter him for his foreign Grand Prix debut at Assen, where we both actually got injured: I broke my leg and he broke his pelvis. Nevertheless he was back three weeks later, racing at Snetterton, where despite jarring his pelvis again in a practice crash on the Friday, he beat Keith Huewen to the Superstock win and finished second behind Roger Burnett in the Race of the Aces. The kid was incredible. I put him forward for the Match Races and again he didn't let me down, qualifying on pole at Brands Hatch, and he was only narrowly beaten for seventh place by Niall Mackenzie in the British Grand Prix at Silverstone. Eventually Kenny wrapped up the Superstock championship in the final round at Brands Hatch, which also happened to be my official retirement from racing in the UK, so you can imagine the size of the party we had.

We were all on a huge high that winter and Kenny and I were getting on really well, so naturally I was keen to sign him up on a proper deal. I remember we had a big meeting down at Heathrow with Geoff Bennett from Loctite and Andy Smith from Yamaha and we did everything we could to tie Kenny down, offering a fully-backed ride with Loctite in the UK and selected rounds of the 500cc World Championship on a Lucky Strike Yamaha. We really thought we had a deal all sewn up but at the last minute Heron Suzuki came in with a big offer for him to go and ride in the F1 World Championship (which would become World Superbikes the following year). It was a contract we couldn't match and an opportunity for Kenny that I didn't begrudge him, but I really was mortified to lose him.

In the end I signed Keith Huewen, a guy with a great pedigree whom I knew well, and even though Keith was a little past his sell-by date we stuck him on our Yamaha and with a bit of support he was able to go and win the title for us again. Alongside Keith I also picked up a kid called Trevor Nation, although it was obvious to both of us that Trevor wasn't my first choice and we never really got on. He spent the whole season trying to make the Yamaha feel like a Suzuki, which is the bike he was used to riding, the results didn't come, and that was the beginning of the end of our relationship. We even gave Trevor's bike to Keith for the penultimate round at Cadwell Park because Keith had destroyed his in a crash during practice. That went down like a shit sandwich with Trevor but we already knew his time with us was coming to an end anyway and it was enough for Keith to clinch the championship for the team for the second successive year.

Meanwhile, the last ever year of the F1 World Championship was won by a guy called Virginio Ferrari on a Bimota, which was an Italian bike powered by a Yamaha engine, so for the 1988 season Mitsui, who were the UK importers for Yamaha, offered us the opportunity to run them in the UK. It seemed like the logical choice so we happily agreed to take on two Bimota YB1s, with FZ750 engines, for the British Championship and selected rounds of the newly-renamed World Superbike series.

The revolutionary thing about the Bimota was that it was the first proper race motorcycle to come with fuel injection, which by now was standard technology for cars. The Italians had designed a system that went onto the Yamaha engine but, like a lot of new technologies, when this system was good it was very, very good and when it was bad it was awful. The season wasn't going well and we were having all sorts of problems when we got to Cadwell Park, where Keith had yet another issue on the warm-up lap. The fuel injection cut out on the Park Straight and Kenny Irons, who had himself not been having a great time with Suzuki, clipped the back of Keith's bike and was sent sliding straight down the track. Another rider came flying through from nowhere and not seeing Kenny lying on the track he ran straight into him.

To be honest I hadn't seen much of Kenny since he left the team and our friendship had been stretched a little bit by the move to Heron Suzuki, but I was still very fond of him. The World Superbike thing hadn't really worked out for him and he was back racing in the UK, arguably wishing he'd stuck with us. Whichever way you look at it, his death was a desperate tragedy and we lost a talent that I think had every possibility to go on and be as successful as the likes of Niall Mackenzie or even Carl Fogarty, the standout British talents of that time. Kenny was funny, interesting, really neat and tidy on the bike, and he was gutsy too. The kid had the whole package and, for me, he was as good as anything there was during that period. Losing him was a blow to the whole British motorcycle industry.

Even though I was now retired from racing, my approach to death at that point still hadn't really changed. I was still in that weird, emotionally dismissive mindset, and maybe because it was one of my bikes that ultimately caused Kenny's death, and I was so fond of the kid, the self-preservation mechanism probably kicked in even more. What I did do, much to the disgust of one or two people in the team and particularly Yamaha, who were selling the bikes, was refuse to run Bimota's fuel injection system any longer. Kenny's death had been a nightmare for our whole team because we still loved him dearly and even though it was nobody's fault we knew we had triggered the whole incident. So we took the bikes back to the workshops, stripped them down and started afresh.

Racing alongside Keith in 1988, I'd hired another promising youngster called Mark Phillips, who had impressed me two years previously when he won the British TTF1 Championship on a two-stroke RG500. Mark had the potential to be very good, although our relationship would eventually go sour sometime after a big crash in an international meeting at Donington Park. One of my mechanics had made a mistake, working under pressure when Mark came in for some new brake pads with five minutes of practice left. The guy didn't put the retaining pin for the brake pads in correctly and they fell out, causing Mark to run straight at the Melbourne Loop. In truth it was one of the best places in the whole of the UK for that to happen because in that particular corner there's around 150 yards of run-off and if Mark had laid the bike down in the gravel, which I would have instinctively done at that point, he'd have probably walked away. But he chose to try and stay on the bike, which was a bad decision, and he rode straight through the gravel trap and hit the barriers. It was a big crash and he was lucky to come away with just a broken arm and a broken leg, although it did put him out for the rest of the season.

It wasn't a good time for Keith either and at the end of the year he actually retired from racing. By then I had already lined up his replacement, a 22-year-old from Kent by the name of Terry Rymer, who had initially impressed me at the first round of the 1987 Superstock season when he blew Keith and Trevor Nation into the weeds around the Brands Indy circuit. Terry was a club racer then and nobody had ever even heard of the bloke, yet he came out on a Yamaha FZ750 that he and his dad had built and blitzed my semi-factory supported riders. 'Too Tall Tel', as we called him, looked too big to be a racer but he didn't half make up for his extra size and weight by riding the bike so hard. He was a gentleman too and proved to be a brilliant signing for us in 1989, bringing the British Superstock Championship back to the team while also becoming the first-ever British rider to win a World Superbike event, with a superb ride at Manfeild in New Zealand, taking the victory ahead of two eventual WSBK legends in Aaron Slight and Fred Merkel.

Terry Rymer – Loctite Yamaha 1989–1991

I was going to watch the likes of Sheene, Grant and Parrish from the age of six or seven with my dad. We'd go to the Grand Prix or the Transatlantic Match Races at Brands Hatch and Silverstone and obviously Sheene was the icon. I actually met him in Australia when I went over there to race in the Swann series in 1988 and Barry must have mentioned to Steve that I was riding well out there. Steve signed me up for Loctite Yamaha and I realised it was going to be a lot of fun from the very first test at Jerez, when we drove down to Spain in the team's big horsebox. The horsebox had living accommodation behind the cab so to cut the boredom we would take turns sitting backwards at the wheel, using this big mirror in the living area to drive the truck. We damn near turned it over a couple of times. That was the start of my education riding for Steve! I was just a kid from a council estate in London, I knew nothing about life in the big wide world, so Steve taught me a lot – starting with all the shortcuts and scams in racing. It was a real baptism of fire. I remember one of the first times we went to Spain, I turned my nose up at the food because I was strictly meat and two veg. So Steve said: 'Bollocks to you then, you're not eating.' It sounds crazy now but all that stuff opened my eyes. We got on well and even though I had an idea about how to set my bike up and stuff, he taught me a lot of extra things. We had a great first season together and I remember when going over to New Zealand we stopped off at Oran Park in Australia for a test. I had raced there before and got my arse kicked by the likes of Mick Doohan, Robbie Phillis, Daryl Beattie and Mal Campbell, so I was determined to make up for that and I was quickly on the pace. We went on to Manfeild, which was tight and twisty, a real scratcher track similar to what I was used to in the UK, and I got on well with it. I won the first race and got a podium in the second one, which was amazing for a private team. We beat some big names and it proved to be one of the best results that the team ever had. Personally, I look back on the three years I had with Steve as three of the best of my career.

Given what had happened to Mark Phillips, and the fact that he'd been faster than Keith before his accident, I had decided to give him another opportunity to ride alongside Terry once he'd recovered, and he did well, winning a few British Champion-ship races during 1989. I was planning to give him a further year until I got a call from a top British rider called Rob McElnea, saying he was coming back from Grand Prix and was available. It was a tough situation but for me as a team boss it really was a no-brainer, so I had to make the decision to let Mark go. Shortly after that I got a letter arriving on my mat from Mark's solici-tors, claiming damages related to his accident.

To say I was surprised is an understatement. These things can happen in racing and, generally, it is an accepted part of the business we are in. At the time, Mark had forgiven the mechanic and of course had been happy to come back and race for me again in 1989. I had helped him a lot, I had invited him to stay at my house and I considered him a friend, so obviously I was very shocked when I opened these envelopes containing claims for huge damages.

The solicitors claimed that the crash had ruined Mark's career, mapping out a hypothetical future where he went on to race at the top level of the 500cc World Championship with the likes of Wayne Rainey, Kevin Schwantz and all the rest of them. They estimated the fortune he would have made and came up with this figure of around a million pounds, which they reckoned we owed him. It was absolutely ludicrous and initially I thought it was some kind of wind-up. Maybe Jeremy Beadle was at it again?

But this time there was no Colonel Fudpucker hiding around the corner and I remember sending all the paperwork back to the solicitors with my response, which was a photograph of my bare backside. I went to Yamaha and Loctite, who helped me out a bit with some financial support but essentially said, 'Your team, your problem', which I guess I could understand. I didn't have insurance against this kind of claim, which I now realised was wrong, but I'd never known it to happen before. I went to the Auto-Cycle Union, who worked with a firm of solicitors called Paris & Co., run by a guy called Steve Paris, funnily enough, and we spent hours and hours over the next two years dealing with the whole matter. Eventually we settled out of court for £75,000, which came out of my own personal bank account, along with £25,000 of personal costs, which brought the job to a nice round hundred grand and left a very sour taste in my mouth.

The only good thing to come out of that experience was that I spent so much time fighting my own case – researching liability laws, working out the physical dynamics of such a crash, like braking distance, kinetic energy and things like that – that I was later able to pick up work as an expert witness for motorcycle racing accidents. It is a job I still do to this day and as a trained engineer who typically enjoys the process of solving mechanical problems it is something I find quite fascinating. I suppose it's a bit of a personal quest too, given what happened with Mark Phillips.

Of course, if there is negligence and they have a right to claim then I would be happy to assist them. But if it is one of these 'no win, no fee' lawyers chancing their arm on a bumper pay day, then I see it as my job to use my years of experience and knowledge of this activity to apportion the blame to where it belongs, which is usually with the rider. Most lawyers don't know the front end of a motorcycle from the back, so my input can often be the basis of their case. It is serendipity, I guess, the way it came about, but some twenty-five years later I reckon I have just about made my hundred grand back!

I suppose the whole issue with Mark Phillips was a lesson in human nature but thankfully I had no such trust issues with Terry Rymer or Rob McElnea, who won a title apiece over the next two seasons. The job had become more stressful than I would have liked, but I still made sure I kept a smile on my face and the rest of the team's, usually at the expense of our YTS mechanic Glen Bright. This kid was so green that when we first took him to the Isle of Man his mother sent him off with a week's supply of the only food he would eat: tinned steak and kidney pies. His diet consisted exclusively of these bloody pies, which are probably nice enough with vegetables every now and again, but Glen ate them every evening on their own or with bread. So we went to the local ShopRite and bought in a few tins of Pedigree Chum and then spent a whole evening assiduously removing the labels with a razor blade and switching them over. Poor old Glen looked a little confused when he took his first forkful but bless him, he ate the lot and had beautiful shiny hair for the rest of the week!

I also got Glen with a stage maroon, which I was now becoming a bit of an expert with. I connected this one to the right-hand indicator of his Morris 1100 and hooked it up to a small bag of flour, which I tucked behind his sun visor, like I'd done to Dave Johnson. When he left the workshops at five o'clock to go home a couple of us followed him at a distance in my car. He got to the village junction in Steeple Morden, where we knew he would be turning right towards the next village, Litlington, where he lived, and just before he got to the junction there was a horse coming towards him, so Glen pulled over to the left and waved the horse rider to come through. The lady politely gave a courtesy wave as she passed the car window, at which point Glen put his indicator on to pull back out into the road. The ensuing explosion scared the shit out of the horse, which reared up and almost threw the rider into the next field. She, of course, started shouting and swearing at Glen, who was climbing out of the car in a daze, covered in white powder, with both of them – and probably the horse too – wondering what the hell had just happened!

Apart from the obvious stresses, running a team was great fun and it suited me down to the ground. I had good bikes, good mechanics, good sponsors, we were the best team in the UK and we were winning the title virtually every year. I was dead set on the job and in all honesty I reckon I would probably still be doing it to this day if it wasn't for an unusual opportunity that had first presented itself at Donington Park some years earlier.

10

Lucky trucker

The *Daily Star* – Friday, 15 August 1986

Parrish revving up for revenge

by Dave Fern

STEVE PARRISH, slim, bronzed and athletic, is equally at home at the wheel of his powerful Mercedes truck as aboard the speedy motorcycle he races with great success.

Parrish has been a truck racer since the first event in Britain in 1984. Last year he was second in the Multipart British Truck Grand Prix and this weekend he aims to win the Star-supported event at Silverstone.

Part of Parrish's enjoyment of truckin' is that it provides him with a chance to achieve something he rarely did on two wheels – beat his great friend and rival Barry Sheene, the double 500cc world champion.

Parrish said: 'I have beaten him every time in trucks but as far as I was concerned he was unbeatable on bikes. It's good to race against him again and see him enjoying the sport but I will beat him again this year.'

Sheene will be driving a DAF in the race that counts for points in the European Truck Racing Championship.

Parrish says of truck racing: 'It's the greatest thing to

happen to British motorsport. It gives everyone a chance to get in at the grass roots. I love it.

'Compared to motorcycle racing it's a bit tame – there is so much wrapped around you in the truck cab.

'It's safer and slower, but you have to plan tactics well in advance. With 7½ tonnes to control, it's the thinking man's racing.'

If there was one issue I had with bike racing, I'd say I wasn't quite brave enough. I worked out pretty early on in my career that there was a fair chance of me getting killed on a motorcycle and I always had that thought at the back of my mind. I did crash, of course, just the same as other guys; my average was probably four or five a year and, racing on the circuits we raced on back then, there was always an element of chance as to how that ended up. I've had bikes cartwheel over the top of me, I've hit hay bales instead of Armco barriers, I have gone sliding on my arse past a tree or past a telegraph pole and thought to myself: 'Shit, I was lucky not to hit that!'

There were, and still are, so many factors out of your control. In those days, as I mentioned earlier, seized engines took a lot of riders' lives and obviously the circuits were far more dangerous. There are still some pretty dangerous tracks out there but if you look at the top level, the MotoGP World Championship, the majority of modern circuits have huge run-off areas and the very latest in air-fence technology, which can turn a potentially catastrophic crash into nothing more than a few bumps and bruises. There has also been significant development of the riders' safety equipment, like electronically activated airbags and hi-tech protectors within their leathers, which have come a tremendously long way since we first started wrapping our knees in duct tape and stuffing pieces of foam-backed cardboard down our backs.

But one risk that we will never be able to eradicate from motorcycle racing is that of getting run over by another rider. The most dangerous time for it to happen is shortly after the start, when virtually the whole grid are still quite tightly packed together. That's exactly what happened to the likes of Mick Patrick and Kenny Irons at Cadwell Park and more recently it was the cause of some of the sport's most high-profile deaths such as Craig Jones, Shoya Tomizawa and Marco Simoncelli. It almost happened to me too, at the Transatlantic Challenge meeting at Donington Park in 1984.

I was riding my old TZ500 Yamaha OW53, which my brilliant mechanic Dave Johnson had renamed 'The Slug' because it was so slow, although I doubt Dave had ever seen a slug because he was never one for eating much lettuce (or anything healthy for that matter). The bike was a former semi-factory works machine that had been ridden in Grands Prix by Boet van Dulmen and was then given to Charlie Williams to race at the TT in 1983. It was supposed to go back to Japan after that but Yamaha UK pleaded with the Japanese to keep it over here and I managed to keep it running for a couple of years, thanks largely to all the spare factory parts I was able to inherit from Barry, who ordered ten of everything when he first signed for Yamaha in 1980 and still had most of it in Franco's workshop.

I had won a few races on The Slug in the UK, as well as a 500cc European Championship race at Donington Park. It was a good handling bike with good brakes but it didn't have the horsepower to compete with the RG500 Suzukis, hence the nickname. I actually qualified quite well that weekend at Donington and when the lights went green I got a reasonably good start, slotting in around fourth place behind Joey Dunlop on a big four-stroke Honda. Joey was a hugely talented Northern Irish road racer whom I never really got to know because I could hardly understand a word he said! Seriously, he was a

122

quiet man but ruthlessly effective on a bike, especially around the Isle of Man TT circuit where he remains the most decorated rider, with 26 wins.

Joey had got a good jump off the line but as much of a legend as he was on the roads I knew I was faster than him on the short circuits, so I was following him down Craner Curves, lining up a pass as we came out of the Old Hairpin, when he missed a gear.

When that happens on a big four-stroke the effect is the equivalent of hitting the brakes, and even though I swerved to avoid Joey, we clipped and I was sent skidding straight down the middle of the track. I'm sure that if the circumstances had been different I would have jumped to my feet and maybe even picked the bike up, but Kenny Roberts was right behind me and even an incredibly talented rider like him could do nothing in that situation. Kenny had nowhere to go but straight over the top of my head, leaving a thick black tyre mark on my white AGV helmet as he was also sent flying from his Yamaha, with Randy Mamola then coming in and colliding with Kenny as the carnage multiplied.

I don't remember anything for a good fifteen minutes after that because unsurprisingly I was completely bowled out, but there was an amazing picture taken by one of the marshals of both Kenny and Randy helping the medics carry me away from the scene in a blanket, with a blurred image of Joey in the background speeding past on his next lap. Kenny and Randy both thought I was dead but eventually I came round and asked Kenny over and over again what had happened. Thankfully it had no longer-lasting effects. A few inches lower, or a lesser-quality helmet, and it could have been a completely different story.

Now I can point to that helmet and smile because it is living proof of one of the very few times in my career that I was actually in front of King Kenny Roberts! A few years ago I got Kenny to sign the helmet – on which he daubed 'Kenny was here!' – and put it up for sale at a charity auction. Being the great bloke that he is, Kenny bid for it himself and he ended up paying something like £2,000 to the charity. He tells me that he still has it up on a shelf at home and whenever I see him he loves to remind me that he is responsible for me being as daft as I am.

When it came to racing, I always felt far less vulnerable on four wheels, so it is quite ironic that I had an equally close brush with death in a car, in a fairly innocuous incident in an old Aston Martin DBS, which I had mistakenly bought as an investment. I was driving to Fowlmere aerodrome, where I used to keep my aeroplane, to fly a young lady friend out to Le Touquet, just over the English Channel near Calais, for a fancy lunch. I was doing about 100mph and coming up to a busy T-junction at Flint Cross when I went to put the brakes on. The old DBS was heated internally by a hot water system, which was powered by a hose that ran under the dashboard, and I must have hit the brakes so hard that the hose burst and blew boiling hot water all over my feet. It was absolutely excruciating and naturally I tucked my knees up and pulled my feet out of the way.

Hurtling towards the upcoming junction at about 70mph, I wasn't left with much choice but to shove my feet back under this boiling spray and I started banging the brakes alternately with my left and then my right foot, finally getting the car stopped just before it careered into the path of the busy oncoming traffic. It was too late to save my poor feet though and instead of spending that afternoon sipping wine and eating fancy French food with a fit bird in Le Touquet, I was sitting at home on the sofa, up to my knees in a bucket of cold water trying to ease the blisters.

Motorcycle racing furnished me with a few other battle scars over the years; I smashed my ankle pretty badly and broke my leg, wrist, collarbone and a few other bits and pieces, but nothing really serious. On the whole I'd say I got away pretty lucky, but I think deep down I was always a self-preservationist, riding slightly within the limits, which for a motorcycle racer in the seventies and eighties was not likely to win you a World Championship. Some of my fellow competitors were of a different mindset and clearly the likes of Kenny or Barry were of that breed. Barry was faster than me on a motorcycle and I can admit that quite happily, but if only he were here right now I'm sure he would tell you that I could kick his arse in a car.

Maybe it was all of those years growing up thrashing old bangers around the airfield as a kid back in Steeple Morden, or maybe it was just the extra safety of being surrounded by a cage that helped me push to the limit without fear, but whenever I took any kind of car on a track I was on lap record pace. I'm not being big-headed, but I genuinely believe that I would have had a more successful career in racing if I'd have switched to four wheels early on. But bikes were cheaper, all my mates had them and it seemed like the natural thing to do when we came up with our plan for Pourus Racing down at the Coach and Horses. Car racing, as far as we were concerned, was for rich people.

However, I remember an occasion in the early nineties when Terry Rymer and I were invited by *Motoring News* to go to Northampton International Raceway at Brafield for a feature on stock cars. They wanted a couple of bike racers to drive the World Champion's car and I got faster and faster until, by the end of the day, I was half a second quicker than him. The team were keen for me to go racing with them but by then I really didn't have the time. I was already too busy running my race team, and I was starting to get serious about a different kind of racing, which once again I had been introduced to by Barry Sheene.

For the last few years of his career, Barry had been sponsored by DAF trucks, so when a marketing guy at Multipart came up with this crazy idea of holding a one-off exhibition race to promote their products, they naturally asked Barry to drive one. As soon as he told me about it I thought 'I fancy a go at that!' so I went to Mercedes and said: 'Barry Sheene is driving in this event for DAF. Do you fancy giving me a truck to race him with?' They loved the idea, quickly sorted out a sponsor, and even though we didn't know it at the time it would prove to be the start of an unbelievably successful relationship.

The first ever Multipart Truck Grand Prix was held at Donington Park on 29–30 September 1984 and it certainly grabbed the imagination of the public. It was all backed by BBC Radio 1, which I know is still quite a popular station (it won't surprise you to hear I am very much a Radio 2 man nowadays) but back then every man and his dog was listening to Radio 1 and Mike Smith, the station's famous DJ, would be taking part in the race – along with Barry and me, of course, and a bunch of other famous drivers like F1 star Martin Brundle, World Rally Champion Stig Blomqvist and multiple Hot Rod World Champion Barry 'Leapy' Lee. They reckoned around 130,000 people turned up to watch the racing that weekend at Donington, which wouldn't surprise me because the traffic brought the M1 and the M6 to a total standstill and East Midlands airport had to be temporarily closed because the emergency vehicles couldn't get through. There had never been anything like it there before and I'm not sure there ever has been since.

I already knew I was pretty good on four wheels but what I didn't expect was just how much of an affinity there would be between riding motorcycles and driving trucks. On a motorcycle everything has to be nice and easy and precise because you don't have a lot of grip. You only have two wheels, and the contact patch between the tyres and the tarmac is about the width of a credit card, so smoothness is key to keeping everything in line. It turned out that racing a truck was very much the same. Whereas a Formula 1 car, which I had tried a couple of times, was all about being aggressive with the steering and using the grip from the tyres to pull the car around the corner, you can't force a truck to do anything because it is way too heavy and there is already so much kinetic energy at work that the tyres cannot counter. You have to coax it, be gentle, anticipate the next move and use natural momentum to guide the load through the turns, just like you do on a motorcycle. Normally, if you see a bike and it looks out of control, sooner or later you can bet it will crash. With the notable exception of guys like Marc Márquez or Casey Stoner, who it must be said are prone to the odd tumble, fast motorcycle racers tend to be silky smooth, and I worked out pretty quickly that it was also the key to getting the maximum speed out of a HGV.

I made it through to the Grand Final of that inaugural event at Donington and I was running second behind the eventual winner Duilio Ghislotti in his Volvo F12 when I had a front tyre blow-out and ran straight into Redgate corner. But even though I didn't make the finish I had taken pretty well to this exciting new sport and as interest grew in staging some more events, and eventually an FIA-sanctioned European Championship, over the coming years I was fortunate enough to be invited back.

During its formative seasons the British Championship was only three or four rounds long and I used to go along in my big Mercedes with sponsorship from BP and clean up. I managed to win a title even by missing the odd race, picking up enough points in the events I did contest to outscore everybody else. In those early days the other competitors tended to be truckers with no racing experience or racers with no trucking experience, like me and my Mercedes UK teammate 'Leapy' Lee, who started racing as a jockey and then as a speedway rider. It was a bit of a giggle, some cash in hand and something to do on the weekends when my Loctite Yamaha team weren't racing.

Truck racing was also perfect for television, especially because we could have a laugh with it and nobody was taking anything too seriously. For one of the races Anglia TV even rigged my cab up with a few cameras and wired me up with a live microphone and earpiece, so that I could talk while the race was going on. Since Leapy was racing in a different category, he was able to go up to the booth and partner Chris Carter as co-commentator. It happened to be pissing down with rain that day and the start of the race was carnage. After a couple of laps my mirrors were all bent in so I couldn't see what was going on behind me and with the amount of spray on the track I could hardly see a thing out of the front either.

Eventually I got in the lead and opened up a bit of a gap but then somebody, one of the Italian drivers I think, started to close in. From his vantage point up in the control tower Leapy could see everything, so he started giving me instructions. I was going, 'Where is he now?' and Leapy would be saying: 'He's on your right! Now swerve left!' The bloke I was racing must have wondered how on earth I was doing it and even though it might not have been strictly within the rules of fair sportsmanship it was making great television and I even managed to win the race! We did a few more of those kind of commentaries and it was tremendous fun.

I managed a couple of other firsts around that time too, like winning a car race and a truck race in the same day. The marketing people at BP felt that for the money they were paying me they needed to get more exposure. So they bought a Caterham and painted it up in BP colours and on the weekends I wasn't racing their truck I was racing their car. On the one weekend that the two series clashed, with the Caterhams at Donington

Park and the trucks at Mallory Park, I won the car race in the morning, jumped on my *CHiPS* police motorbike, which had a siren on it and flashing lights, raced down to Mallory and won there in the afternoon! Incidentally I sold that motorcycle to Jay Kay from Jamiroquai. He came to an event called Race Retro at Stoneleigh Park and foolishly said, 'Whose is that? I've got to have it!' so I bumped the price up by a few quid and had it delivered to his house.

It was while I was racing Caterhams that I also set the world record for reversing. They built me a special car with altered geometry and six reverse gears and we went to Bruntingthorpe airfield, where I managed to do 89mph backwards. Everybody thought I was completely mad but I had actually gained some experience of the discipline some years earlier, in an old Rover SD1 V8 that I picked up from *Exchange and Mart* in London. I was driving it through the centre of Buntingford when I had to stop and reverse because there was a lorry coming in the other direction and there wasn't enough room for us both to get through. With a few bystanders looking on I put the thing into reverse and floored the throttle in an effort to spin the tyres up and look cool. But this old thing was such a pile of crap that the engine mountings broke and the whole engine twisted in the engine compartment and jammed the throttle flat out. The front wheels locked up with the back wheels spinning and pouring with smoke as I went careering down Buntingford High Street at about 50mph in reverse. People were jumping for cover but I managed to switch the ignition off before anybody got hurt and it proved to be good training for my world record attempt.

The other thing that really suited me about racing cars and trucks was the amount of cheating that was going on, which I have always been something of an expert at. In the early days of truck racing we were just designated a category according to the truck's horsepower and given a big sticker to put on the side, but we were all pretty much lying so they started to run checks. On arrival at the track the trucks would be measured for horsepower on a rolling road, which is like a big dyno, and then assigned to the relevant category for that weekend's races.

Now, the easiest way to get a truck to go faster is just to get more fuel into the engine. In a diesel engine the fuel is pumped in with an injector and if you can just get a little more fuel in you can turbocharge more air, so that it builds up the power. So we had our trucks fitted with these little solenoid switches that opened up the pumps and gave you a sudden blast of power. In my truck, which still had a stereo in it, we hooked up the electrics so that I could simply turn the radio on and suddenly gain another hundred horsepower. Others had even craftier ideas, like Richard Walker, who carried the truck's cigarette lighter around in his pocket so nobody knew what he was doing, but once he got in the truck he could plug it in and suddenly ramp up the power. You always knew what was going on because you'd be bombing around Silverstone on the first lap and then all of a sudden you'd see somebody fiddling around and the next thing there'd be plumes of black smoke and they'd go tearing off like a scalded cat. There really was so much cheating going on in those early days with the speed limiters and the fuelling and everything else, but to me it was all part of the fun.

I got a further opportunity to exploit my craft during the early nineties when I was invited to take part in a challenge for a big Saturday evening television show called *You Bet!*, which was hosted by Matthew Kelly. The idea of the show was that a panel of celebrities would bet on whether or not somebody could complete a particular challenge. The studio audience also cast their vote and the celebrity would be awarded points for each outcome they predicted correctly, based on the percentage of the studio audience that also placed a correct bet. The challenge I was put forward for was to drive my race truck blindfolded around Mallory Park, with a knob on the steering wheel and long-haired team manager Dave Atkins giving me instructions according to the numbers on a clock face, like: 'Three o'clock, two o'clock, eleven o'clock . . . nine!'

The challenge was to complete a lap within 90 per cent of my normal fastest time, which would have been pretty bloody impossible, not to mention dangerous, if I didn't cheat a bit. Luckily, with my nose being so big, it lifted the blindfold slightly so that I could see just enough of the track to get my bearings and not smash into the barriers! Of course, I managed to complete the lap within the time limit and the producers loved it so much that we decided to see if I could do it again – this time in my aeroplane. I would have to take off and land at Fowlmere aerodrome with a blindfold on and just an instructor from the flying club talking me through the procedures. Once again my large hooter came in handy and I miraculously managed to complete another challenge!

This remarkable run of daredevil achievements finally came to an end when they foolishly dared me to a third challenge: a slalom race in my Mercedes sports car against one of the top polo ponies in the country! The race would take place on a grass polo pitch, where they set out two identical rows of poles and gave us a couple of practice runs to get used to the course. The horse won each time because the ground was a little soft and it could turn much quicker than I could in the car, so when we did it for real I beeped the horn halfway through and the poor horse bolted off in the opposite direction! Unsurprisingly, that proved to be my last *You Bet!* challenge but at least I maintained my 100 per cent record, and I still have the trophies to prove it.

11

Trucking idiots

My team were, quite literally, a bunch of trucking idiots really and how we won so many races I'm not sure. They were run out of Mansfield by a guy called Dave Atkins, who got involved with me in the very early days. Dave had long hair and he dressed like a hippy but he was no fool; he had a fuel injection business and somehow managed to talk BP into giving us so much bloody money, about a million pounds a year, to run the team. The mechanics were all in it for the piss-up really; I'd turn up at the track for practice in the morning and there'd be beer bottles all over the place, everybody fast asleep. But they'd get up and fix up the truck and for the first few years we just went out and kicked everybody's arse.

It wasn't long before truck racing became a serious business and by 1990 I found myself part of a twelve-round FIA championship, taking in many of the same circuits as Formula 1 – like Silverstone, Hockenheim, the Nürburgring and Paul Ricard. All across the continent the crowds were huge, averaging 100,000 and above at most venues and up to 168,000 at the Nürburgring, the home round for the two main manufacturers – Mercedes and MAN. I'd never seen anything like it in all my days racing motorcycles. What started out as a bit of fun back in the mid-eighties was now a full-on factory sport, with our effort being officially run by Mercedes Germany. We were driving millions of pounds' worth of kit, with backroom staff, crew and hundreds of spare parts. The board of Mercedes were coming along to the races and there was a team of 50 people back at the factory working on the project. The truck racing team ran on the same budget as the DTM team and it was every bit as important to Mercedes.

Back home I was still running my Loctite Yamaha team but it was getting awkward with Mercedes because I was ducking and diving a bit, missing races in both championships and not really doing either of them justice. I still managed to win the main Super-Race-Truck class title in 1990 but in 1991 I lost out to a German called Gerd Körber, who drove for MAN, and eventually Mercedes told me that it was time to choose: bikes or trucks. It wasn't a hard decision to make. I loved running my team but the urge to compete still ran deep in my veins. I knew I could run a team forever if that's what I wanted to do, but I couldn't keep on racing and this might be my last opportunity.

I called a meeting at my house in Royston at the end of 1991 with Andy Smith and Ray Ross from Yamaha UK and we all agreed we needed to make a decision. Before they fired me, I agreed to close up the workshops and become a full-time racer again. Conveniently, Rob McElnea had his mind set on the idea of running a team himself, so he effectively inherited the Loctite sponsorship, took my bikes and my mechanics and signed James Whitham to run alongside him. It was a shrewd signing by Rob because James had a long relationship with Suzuki and Mick Grant and in my view he had long been one of the most promising young riders in the paddock. I would get to work with him later in life as part of the Isle of Man TT commentary team and would experience his honesty and hilarious Yorkshire wit as a colleague.

James is also tough as old boots and unfortunately he knocked Rob off at Mallory Park: the injuries he sustained effectively ended Rob's career as a rider, although he went on to prove himself as a very capable team manager. And much like me with Loctite, Rob later secured a sponsor whose products he got great satisfaction from, it's fair to say: he did a deal with Cadbury's Boost!

Meanwhile, I became a full-time professional truck racer, signing a contract with Mercedes that was worth three times more than I had ever earned as a bike racer and being treated in a way I certainly had not been accustomed to. I would be getting flown to races, rather than travelling in the van with the mechanics like I had done throughout my bike racing career, and they even gave me a new car and paid for my petrol! It would turn out to be the best career move I ever made.

The trucks had also moved on a great deal from the slightly modified road vehicles that I had started out driving some eight years earlier. The factory Mercedes Actros 1450 S was a 12-litre V6 that in standard spec would produce about 450 horsepower, although these guys were working miracles by getting it up to something like 2,000 horsepower. Even with a minimum weight of five tonnes the thing was a bloody rocket ship that went from 0–100mph in 9.6 seconds. To keep the brakes from overheating under that much stress they developed a system to spray them with water and during a single race we could easily use 85 litres. If the water ran out, you had about one lap left in your brakes. All that information, all those forces on the brakes and suspension, was incredibly useful for the factories and also the sponsors, who tended to be major oil, tyre or engineering companies. They could learn more from a thirty-minute truck race than they could from a month's development at their laboratories or test facilities, so along with the great publicity the sport was getting at the time it is no wonder it became so important to them.

If you ever came across one of these weapons on a public road then you'd have got the shock of your life. That's exactly what happened to some flashy Porsche driver when we snuck out of the paddock at the Nürburgring during a race weekend to test the truck, which had been cutting out during practice. This bloke tried to overtake me, so I put my foot down and almost blew him into the hard shoulder. He turned out to be one of the German race directors and I got properly busted, with the police involved and everything, because obviously the truck had no plates on it and wasn't road legal. Testing on the public roads around the circuit was very much outside the judicial and moral boundaries of the sport but fortunately, because we were in Germany, the bosses at Mercedes somehow got it all squashed.

Mercedes had allowed me to keep my team together, with Dave Atkins and all the boys, and somehow we continued our winning streak at the highest level. We won the Super-Race-Truck category four more times between 1992 and 1996 – it was amazing really; a long-haired hippy, a bunch of drunk mechanics and a washed-up motorcycle racer and we were smoking the factory drivers. All these German teams would turn up, as you can imagine, in their freshly-ironed uniforms with their shiny shoes, and they couldn't understand how we kept beating them. In all honesty, I wasn't really sure myself.

The racing was serious but I still managed to keep myself entertained, stitching up my mechanics and the other drivers wherever possible. One of the drivers I got on particularly well with was a guy called George Allen, a proper trucker who owned a chassis alignment company called Truckline. Obviously George wasn't stupid because the European Truck Racing Championship paddock was a gold mine for his business; and he always liked having a giggle, so we became good mates. So when I found a dead snake in the paddock at Paul Ricard, I didn't think twice about getting him with it.

Unlike most of us, who got all our gear on before the sighting lap, George had a little hook on his roll cage where he hung his helmet, gloves and everything else, and he would wait until we were all on the grid ready to race before putting it all on. Once the sighting lap was over, I parked next to him on the grid and when he nipped off for his pre-race comfort break, I made my move. The snake must have been pretty fresh because it didn't look dead at all – well, snakes don't really ever look all that alive, do they? – and it was quite a big bastard, because even curled up it only just fitted inside George's helmet.

I could barely handle the tension on the grid that day, not because I was nervous about the race but because I couldn't wait to see George's reaction when he saw the snake. I didn't have to wait too long because no sooner had the five-minute board gone up than the door of his cab flew open, followed by George himself, hanging half-upside-down as he thrashed about frantically trying to free himself from his harness. The poor bastard was screaming and kicking his legs with the bloody snake still draped across his lap! Poor George. I genuinely had no idea that he had a phobia of snakes; nobody had told me and I had no reason to suspect it. Why would I? He damned near had a heart attack and, if I remember correctly, I don't think he was able to make the start of the race.

I felt bad about that one, but I have absolutely no regrets about a prank I pulled on one of the other drivers, Helmut Kruger, a rich German knob who bought himself an ex-factory Mercedes truck. He was absolutely useless – the guy couldn't drive a greasy stick up a cow's arse – but the truck was a rocket ship so he was always just a complete pain in the neck, constantly crashing into people because he couldn't stop for corners. I remember a race at Dijon when I was lapping him and the bloody idiot still smashed into the back of me and rammed me off the track. He was a Helmut by name, and a massive helmet by nature.

Often we would be called into driver briefings before a race, the FIA Steward dishing out a general reprimand because there had been so many crashes in practice, which was usually all down to Helmut. But they didn't seem to want to take specific action against him, so I decided to take matters into my own hands and during yet another one of these unnecessary briefings I grabbed hold of his helmet, smothered the inside with Loctite, knowing full well that the bastard wore a wig, and shoved it back under his chair.

At the end of the race I was due up on the podium but I didn't want to go up there until I had seen Helmut take his helmet off. To my great joy, as he pulled it off he must have realised the syrup was coming with it, so he clamped it back down again and stormed off in a huff. Like some of my best work I never got to see the full extent of the damage, but I didn't need to. That one was just perfect as it was.

There were a few other drivers we didn't like and there was a very easy way to make sure they had a shitty end to the weekend. Nearly all of them had motorhomes, and as anybody who has one of these vehicles will know, they have a stopcock and a cap over the end of the toilet outlet. The idea is that when you want to empty it out you can put a pipe over the end and dispose of any waste properly in the appropriate place. But I used to have great fun creeping around at night, moving the stopcocks around a notch and then screwing the caps back on over the top, so that as soon as the unsuspecting owner unscrewed the cap it would spray out everywhere and cover them in shite.

That was one of many tricks I played on Alan Clarke, who was our team truck driver and a talented guitarist who often provided the entertainment, in more ways than one. Alan was a great sport who would do anything if we paid him and one of his finest moments was at one of my championship presentation dinners, when Richard Walker and I gave him a tenner each to walk behind the top table, which was full of FIA Stewards, completely bollock naked. Another beauty I played on Alan was at Brands Hatch, when I got hold of his bicycle and hacksawed it almost completely in half. He used to like to go cycling first thing in the morning so we all got up early to watch him off. The bike was just about held together by the clips that keep the cables in place but with the first strong push on the pedals the whole thing fell apart. Poor Alan was lying upside down with the handlebars still in his hands – he didn't know what the hell had just happened!

Eventually Alan got his own back by getting hold of my golf clubs and hacksawing through the shafts beneath the grips, carefully putting them all back together and placing them back in my bag. My next game of golf happened to be a big charity affair so I was teeing off at the first with tons of people standing around watching when my driver just flew out of my hands. I excused myself and pulled out the three wood but, of course, exactly the same thing happened again! The bastard had been through every single club in the bag.

One morning at Mantorp Park in Sweden the rest of the mechanics had colluded to get me and I was just pulling into the paddock when I saw a full effigy – my overalls, boots and gloves, all stuffed with straw, and my helmet with a banana sticking out – hanging from a crane with a noose around the neck! The Germans must have been looking at us like we were completely mad but I took it all down, gave it a clean and then went out and won the race.

One of the guys, a data logging engineer from Cambridge called Mark Harrington, was given the nickname Virgil because when he got drunk, as in every weekend, he walked just like the character from *Thunderbirds*. On the morning after a race in Dijon, France, I was flying back to the UK with one of the other drivers, the former ABBA drummer Slim Borgudd, and I offered Virgil a lift. As usual, he had a hangover so he was fast asleep for the whole flight, snoring, dribbling and farting in the back of the plane. As we came over the English Channel at about 4,000 feet I said to Slim, 'Watch this', and put the plane into a dive, heading straight for the Sealink Ferry. Slim leans into the back and shouts: 'Get out! Get out!' Poor Virgil almost shat his pants – he actually tried to unbuckle himself and jump out of the plane! Strangely enough, he stayed awake for the rest of the trip.

Slim Borgudd was a really pleasant old boy, slim by name and nature with thinning blonde locks, who had made a load of money through music and then pretty much blown it all, as far as I know, on motor racing, although he was certainly no mug behind a steering wheel. He had years of experience in touring cars and had even done a couple of seasons in Formula 1, so he was a really strong competitor and actually beat me to the title in 1995. Slim was a good friend but my real nemesis back then was Gerd Körber, who believe it or not is still racing trucks to this day. In 1991 he was the new up and coming talent, and we went into the Nürburgring race battling for the championship. It was the biggest event of the year and with me driving for Mercedes and Körber for the factory's main competition MAN, there was a huge rivalry brewing on all parts.

As usual, there were 160,000 fans there, including the big boss of Mercedes, Helmut Werner, who was so important and so highly regarded by the German government that he was one of the only people in the country allowed to have an armed bodyguard permanently by his side. It turned out that this hired gunman was actually English, ex-SAS no less, so I managed to get chatting with him and we got on pretty well, which would come in handy later.

Mr Werner's kids loved truck racing so he'd helicoptered the whole family into the Nürburgring. Obviously I was as nice as pie with his kids, giving them stickers and posters and even these little remote control replicas of my truck that had been made – so Mr Werner was right on my side. Before the race started he came up to me and said: 'Today you have to win, Steve. My kids would really like that. Also, this is a big deal for Mercedes.' He even offered me a little bonus, which was this incredibly trick miniature Mercedes SL with a petrol engine that they made for children, which he promised to send over to my house for Frankie.

By now the trucks were pretty much full-blown prototypes. A bit like Superbikes, they were supposed to be modified pro-duction models but all the factories did was market them in brochures as 'fast response vehicles' for airports, which they never sold a single unit of. And I knew I had a big problem because MAN had brought some quite significant upgrades that weekend and Körber had been lapping a second quicker than me in practice. Gerd was a good driver and we shared a mutual, respectful, dislike for each other. It was always him and I knocking the shit out of each other on track and we were always getting hauled in front of the stewards for something or other. But I knew that this race would have to top anything we'd ever done before if I was going to get Frankie in that little Merc.

The race started and I managed to slam my truck down the inside of Körber at turn one, sliding it all the way in and slotting into the lead. For the next 18 laps I pulled every single trick in the book to keep that bastard behind me. It was like Valentino Rossi versus Casey Stoner at Laguna Seca in 2008.

Wherever Körber wanted to be on the track, I made sure I was there. He pushed and shoved to try and find a way past and by the time we got to the end of the race both the back of my truck and the front of his were absolutely beaten to shit. Körber went absolutely ballistic, making an official complaint to the stewards and everything, but of course we both knew they were never going to take a win off Mercedes at the Nürburgring; there'd have been a riot.

Yet still Körber was absolutely fucking furious so he came charging around to my garage with all his big burly mechanics for a proper sort out. Luckily, I saw them coming so I grabbed the SAS guy from Mr Werner and said: 'Here you are mate – I've got a job for you!' Körber's cronies took one look at this bloke, stopped in their tracks and promptly fucked off. It was so cool; not only did Frankie get the car, but I got an upgrade on mine – as well as another contract for the next season! It was just a shame I didn't have that bodyguard with me the rest of the time because I could have certainly done with him later that season in Finland, when a nice quiet evening on a picturesque lake somehow, once again, turned into yet another close call.

The PR manager for our main sponsor, BP Commercial Oils, was a lovely lady called Dorothy Boothroyd, a well-spoken ex-public schoolgirl and staunch patriot whose most important day of the year was St George's Day. Dorothy came to the races and, since she looked after the budget, always made sure we stayed in nice hotels and ate in fancy restaurants. One evening we arrived early for dinner at this place on the edge of a beautiful lake near the track at Alastaro. There were a couple of rowing boats tied to a jetty next to the restaurant, so assuming that they belonged to the proprietors a few of us thought we'd take them for a little row around the lake and work up an appetite. I was in one boat with Dorothy and Dave

Atkins, and Alan Clarke was in another with a Czechoslovakian mechanic called Jiří Moskal.

After a nice, peaceful little bob around the lake we decided to head back to the shore, with Alan getting there first, some way ahead of us. We could see that his arrival had caused some kind of commotion and as we got closer to the edge of the water it looked as if there was a bloody shark attack going on. Alan had been hauled out of his boat by this 6' 6" monster of a Finnish bloke, who was going absolutely berserk, shouting obscenities in Finnish and dunking him under the water trying to drown him! Jiří was a big lad himself but even he was swinging from this bloke's neck, trying to punch him but making hardly any difference at all. Part of me wanted to row as hard as I could in the opposite direction but there was obviously no way we could leave Alan like that because there'd have been nobody to drive the trucks home.

Dave fancied it about as much as me but we jumped out of our boat, splashed over there and piled in. We managed to restrain the guy just enough for Alan to catch his breath, until finally I picked up an oar that had floated my way. Jiří jumped out of the way as I swung for this guy and snapped the oar clean in two pieces over his enormous back. Like some kind of baddie from a Bond movie, the guy just turned around slowly and stared at me in a trance-like state of calm fury. That moment of stillness in time gave us a crucial second or two to make our getaway, and as Jiří split in one direction, Dorothy, Dave, Alan and I went sprinting back to the hotel, where we hid in a broom cupboard while this lunatic went rampaging round the corridors looking for us. Eventually, the police were called and they came and took him away. It turned out he was a local nutcase who was always getting drunk and causing similar chaos.

When I wasn't cowering in a broom cupboard I usually

142

enjoyed visiting Finland, although I got stopped for speeding every year, which was an expensive habit until I realised that the fine was means tested. They gave you a form to fill in which included questions on your income and the size of your family. I would put down that I earned the minimum wage and had six children, so my fine was about a tenner. Meanwhile my teammate at the time, a flashy Frenchman called Ludovic Faure, got stopped on his first trip to Finland and told them that he was 26 years old, earned €150,000 and had no children. The dozy bastard got a bill for about £450!

My truck racing career came to a halt at the end of the 2001 season, when Mercedes took the decision to withdraw from the sport, although not before I managed to get one last juicy contract out of them with a bargaining technique that I think is still unique within motorsport. It was midway through the race at Alastaro in 1999, when my teammate Markus Oest-reich was fighting to win the championship, and a message came over the radio from my crew chief that the Mercedes team manager wanted me to move over. 'No problem,' I told them, 'as long as you agree to the following demands . . .' After a brief negotiation I got the figure I wanted on my new contract and promptly pulled aside to let Markus through.

Racing trucks had been an extension to my racing career that I never expected to happen, and once it did I could never have imagined how successful it would be or how long it would last, with seven British Championships and five World Championships to my name over more than a decade in the sport. Ultimately, though, it always felt like a job and it certainly wasn't the same lifestyle I'd had as a motorcycle racer. The other drivers weren't really the kind of people I was used to hanging about with – the daredevil playboys like Barry Sheene or Piers Weld-Forester – and there wasn't that communal sense of jubilation on a Sunday night at simply having survived to tell another tale. Most people, me included, had a family to go home to and in some cases a full-time job, so everybody just packed up and went home.

With Mercedes gradually ceasing development of their race trucks in the latter years it had become even harder to get excited about racing because our chances of winning were increasingly slim, plus I had started to turn my attentions to another career, which had much brighter long-term prospects. Once again in my life, I found that as one door was starting to close the next one was opening and, once again, I had a quite straightforward decision to make.

12

Doctor Parrish

John Hopkins – MotoGP rider 2002–2011

The Japanese Grand Prix at Motegi had been a really tough weekend for me. I qualified on the front row but got caught up in a huge pile-up in turn one and ended up with three broken ribs, a huge gash in my butt, and I was pretty busted up, so the flight back to London from Narita was never going to be much fun. Usually in those days I always had somebody travelling with me but on that occasion I happened to be on my own. I managed to get myself onto the plane with no issues but my cabin bag was quite heavy, so obviously I couldn't lift it a whole lot. So I asked the stewardess if she could give me a hand. 'No problem,' she said. 'Is everything okay?'

'Well, I've got three broken ribs, so it's not so easy for me to get it up there.' So, no problem, she took over putting the bag away and I took my seat. I was just trying to get comfortable when the stewardess came back with the captain, who said he understood I had three broken ribs and did I have a doctor's note to certify that I could fly? I said: 'No, I didn't assume that I needed one.'

The captain was like: 'Well, I'm sorry sir, but with three broken ribs and no doctor's note there's no way we can let you fly.' I tried telling them that I had spoken with the MotoGP medical staff about it, which I hadn't, although I realised then that I should have. So I just lied and said the doctors had told me I was okay to fly but that now everybody was already on their way back to Europe so there was no way for me to get a note. They weren't buying it and I was really starting to panic that I was going to be kicked off the plane and left there on my own, with all these injuries and nobody to help me get fixed up. I had visions of lying in some hospital bed in Japan for days on end. It was a scary prospect and I was getting desperate. I said: 'Come on guys, there is literally nobody I know in Japan. Everybody is skipping town – to be honest I bet there's even one of our doctors on this flight!'

'I'm one of the doctors,' I lied, springing into action. I'd been watching this whole thing unfold from a couple of seats back and if there is one country I wouldn't want to get left behind in, it's Japan. I've been there plenty of times and it still doesn't make any sense to me: it's like being on Mars. To me the best place in the whole country was the runway out of Narita airport, so now we were on it I had full sympathy for 'Hopper'. Also, as usual, I was thinking of myself and I figured that if he got kicked off this flight we'd be delayed by at least an hour while they located and removed his luggage from the hold. My colleague Charlie Cox and I both had meetings to attend back in London that we really didn't want to miss. 'I have examined Mr Hopkins and he's fine to fly,' I assured the captain.

'You're a doctor are you?' he asked. 'I'm afraid I'll need to see some proof.'

'Yes, of course,' I said, producing my business card: *Steve Parrish N.L.A.M.N, PHD.*

He looked at the card and seemed satisfied, although I'm sure he'd have changed his mind if he'd bothered to ask me what the letters stood for. Personally, I am quite proud of 'No Letters After My Name, Pizza Hut Delivery', but they hardly qualified me to take a medical decision such as this.

'Well then, Doctor Parrish, you wouldn't mind signing a release form so that the gentleman can fly?'

'Of course not,' I replied, as the eyes of the BBC's motor-sport producer Belinda Rogerson started to burn a hole in the side of my head.

The stewardess went off to fetch the form and Belinda went absolutely apeshit. 'Who the hell do you think you are?' she ranted. 'If anything happens on this flight the BBC are going to be liable. There is no fucking way you're going through with this!'

'I fucking am, it's too late now,' I hissed, as the stewardess headed back with the form. I signed it 'Doctor S. Parrish' and took my seat, kicked back and closed my eyes, happy to be heading back to Blighty on schedule.

My sense of self-satisfaction evaporated around two hours into the flight, when an announcement came over the cabin PA: 'Can the doctor on board please make his way to the back of the cabin?'

I couldn't believe it. Surely there was another doctor on board? I ignored the message, but a few moments later there was a hand on my shoulder. 'Doctor Parrish? We've got a problem at the back of the plane. We need some help. Can you follow me?' This couldn't be happening. I virtually soiled myself there and then but fortunately for me I'd watched *Casualty* and *Holby City*. I got up from my seat and followed the steward down the plane to an office. Every row was full of MotoGP team members, riders, mechanics, PR people and journalists, most of them asleep, the awake ones all giving me a confused look. I shrugged and smiled and kept on walking but in my head I was frantically running through my options.

Do I lock myself in the toilet and hide there for the remainder of the flight? Do I come clean and tell them I'm not actually a doctor and I can't help? Or do I just carry on and hope it's not some poor soul having a heart attack or, worse still, a baby? By the time we got to the office I still wasn't sure, but I got a stroke of luck when the stewardess explained the situation. 'We have a passenger causing all sorts of problems at the back of the plane, doctor. He's drunk and being offensive to his fellow passengers and the crew. We need you to examine him and sign him off.'

'Well, to be honest, orthopaedics is more my field,' I replied. 'But on this occasion I'll help you out.'

So we continued down towards the back of the plane and got to about four or five rows away from this drunken fellow – a cameraman from a Spanish television crew that I happened to have done a bit of filming with that weekend.

'Heeeey, Stavros!' he slurred, waving at me with a big grin on his face.

'Well, this man is clearly not with his senses,' I said, checking his pulse and lifting his eyelids. 'But I'm quite happy that he is, as you suspected, just drunk. Give him a glass of water, he'll be fine.'

After 11 hours of purgatory, hoping desperately that nobody else got struck down by illness, we landed at Heathrow, where the captain came down to greet the passengers as they disembarked. He looked at me with a smile, shook my hand and said: 'Love your commentary, Steve.' He knew all along I wasn't a doctor and clearly was in as much of a hurry to get out of Japan as I was! Meanwhile, the poor Spanish cameraman was arrested and missed his connecting flight to Madrid.

I don't think Belinda ever quite saw the funny side of that one either but by this time I had been working with the BBC on and off for over twenty years, so they were well used to having to make excuses for my behaviour. Travelling the world as a television commentator was a career I could never have foreseen back in Mr Caruthers' geography class at The Shrubbery, but somehow it had followed seamlessly on from racing motorcycles and trucks and had become another way to keep me out of the job centre without ever feeling like I'd worked a single day in my life. It's now well over forty years since I left school with nothing and I still have most of it left!

Again, it was a twist of fate that led to the switch from pit-lane to the commentary box, although it didn't seem like a very fortunate one at the time. I entered what would prove to be my final Grand Prix at Silverstone in 1984 as a wildcard on The Slug, with backing from Wrangler Jeans and Mitsui, who were the British importers for Yamaha. Mitsui weren't too bothered about me racing internationally as their business was based entirely in the UK, so I was concentrating mainly on domestic races and just did the odd overseas event, like Macau. Anything extra like that would be at my own expense, so I had to make sure the start money covered the costs.

To be fair, we didn't have any problems with the bike over the weekend, until the start of the race. As usual it was a push start but I pushed and pushed . . . and pushed . . . and the old girl just wouldn't fire up. The rest of the grid tore off into turn one, with Ron Haslam getting the best start to lead a British one-two ahead of Barry. There were some great riders and even greater characters on that grid, including a bunch of American youngsters like Randy Mamola and Eddie Lawson, who had followed in the footsteps of Kenny Roberts and would soon be joined by Wayne Rainey and Kevin Schwantz, to mark a great era in Grand Prix motorcycle racing for the USA. In fact, Randy would go on to win that race, ahead of Eddie and Ron.

But by the time they all blasted past me in that thunderous

cacophony of screaming 500cc two-strokes at the end of their first lap, my own Grand Prix career was over. The Slug had yet to make so much as a splutter and finally I gave up and threw it against the concrete pit wall, climbed over the top into the pit-lane and started the long trudge back towards my awning. Just then a reporter from BBC Radio 2 called Andy Smith came running up with a microphone, asking what had happened. I poured my heart out to him about how distraught I was, the amount of effort that had gone in from the team and the sponsors to get us on the grid for my home round, and how devastating it was for us all to not even make the start. After he switched the mic off, Andy said: 'Crikey Steve, that was pretty concise. You'll have to come and do some work for us.'

So when the British Grand Prix came around again twelve months later, they asked me back to be a pundit alongside their main commentator Nick Harris for the race, which would be broadcast live on *Sport on 2*, the BBC's radio equivalent of *Grandstand*. The programme would cover all the main sporting events of the day, including any major motorcycle races, and for the British Grand Prix they would host the whole programme live from Silverstone. I had known Nick since he was a young journalist knocking on my caravan door for a quote for *Motor Cycle Weekly*, and over the years we had become good friends.

Nick Harris – Motorcycle Grand Prix journalist and BBC reporter

I was well-versed in Steve's ways, having followed him and Barry around the world for the best part of a decade or more for *Motor Cycle Weekly* and *Motor Cycle News*. I actually travelled with them to Daytona one year, which was an absolute bloody nightmare. They were having a long jump competition, driving the hire car off the sea wall onto the beach to see who could go the furthest. Eventually the car blew up in Fort Lauderdale – it was making so much noise we jumped out and crouched in a ditch because we genu-inely thought it was about to explode! Then on the way back Stavros caused a stink at Miami airport when he stole one of those golf carts they use to ferry disabled people around and drove us right up to the gate in it. On the plane, while I was sleeping, he dropped my tray table down and wrote 'I want to fuck you' on it in black marker pen, and then folded it back up again. When the hostess came around to wake me up and ask if I wanted breakfast I nodded and smiled, so she dropped the table down, saw the message and nearly threw my orange juice in my face! The only time I ever tried to get him back, I jacked the rear wheels of his car off the ground, but he just got in it and drove off. It was front wheel drive! I'm just no good at that sort of thing, and soon realised it was better not to get involved. Anyway, the producer of *Sport on 2* was a lady called Pat Thornton, who went on to be a big hitter at the BBC. After the 1987 British Grand Prix, which was held for the first time at Donington Park, she took the whole team out for a congratulatory meal on the Sunday night because it had gone so well. Radio was a big deal back then and there were probably fifteen people working on a live production, so we had this big long table in the conservatory of a restaurant down by a river near the circuit. It was all very pleasant, with everybody patting each other on the back, until Pat stood up and cleared her throat to make a little speech. Unbeknownst to any of us, Stavros had given the waiter a box of chocolates to put out on the table, and just before starting her speech Pat popped one in her mouth. She started talking while chewing this choco-late, at which point a bloody great big condom came sliding

151

out of her mouth! Of course, she didn't have a clue what was happening so she just stood there with a rubber johnny hanging around her chin. Meanwhile Stavros and I were just under the table laughing.

I bought those particular chocolates ready-made from a retired Swiss rider called Philippe Coulon, who was still working in the paddock, but they were really expensive so over the years I have perfected my own recipes, converting Ferrero Rochers by boring out the centre with an apple corer, resealing them and wrapping them back up in the gold foil. I always like to leave a box lying open when we are backstage at the big NEC motorcycle show in November and have caught tons of people out, including the former Eurosport commentator Toby Moody, who once swallowed a condom whole. Thankfully, up until recently, I always had a fresh supply, thanks to a mate of mine who used to work for Durex, although if you are thinking of trying this trick at home I must say it works equally well with dog biscuits or Brussels sprouts. Just be careful not to swap them with granny's Milk Tray at Christmas as, believe me, the results can be catastrophic.

Thankfully Pat Thornton eventually saw the funny side of the incident and it didn't cause too much damage to my chances of further employment with the BBC. Once again I would be the beneficiary of my old mate's slipstream, because when Barry Sheene packed up and jetted off to Australia, he left a gap in the television commentary box that they were eager for me to fill.

I had already been doing some television work with Eurosport around their coverage of the new World Superbike series, commentating on the races with Jack Burnicle from their studios in Paris. Eurosport seemed really happy with what we were doing and in fact were so keen for me to do more that they even offered me my own weekday motorsport show. However, Barry convinced me that an offer from the BBC doesn't come along every day and with my truck racing career starting to wind down I knew it was too good an opportunity to refuse.

Joining the BBC was the best decision I could have made because I would go on to enjoy some of the best years of my life with them, working alongside some fantastically talented colleagues, starting with the legendary Murray Walker. Most people remember Murray for his iconic commentaries on Formula 1 but what a lot of people don't realise is that his first passion is actually motorcycle racing and in particular the Isle of Man TT, where his father Graham raced with some distinction, including a victory in the lightweight class in 1931. After he finished racing Graham took up commentating for BBC radio and he was soon joined by Murray, who carried his books around and I believe actually partnered his dad as a commentator in 1949, which is incredible when you think that he is still doing occasional television work almost seventy years later.

Murray and I would have first met on opposite sides of the microphone when he interviewed me at the British Grand Prix. Back in those days the riders and the press would spend a lot of time together, travelling to the races and such, because the paddock was so much smaller than it is now, and one of my abiding memories of Murray is of teaching him to waterski at Repulse Bay in Hong Kong, where we would go to unwind on the Monday after the Macau Grand Prix. I sat in the water with him, showed him how to get his knees around the waterskis, told him to keep his arms straight and his feet together and let the boat do the work. Good old Murray got up first time, but just as he set off I whipped his trunks down and shouted: 'SHARKS! SHARKS!' So the poor bloke just hung on for dear life with his willy flapping around in the wind.

Mind you, at least it helped him keep his feet together!

By now a rather posh, tall chap called Mark Wilkin was in charge of the bike racing at the BBC and Mark, who did everything with a certain swagger and an air of conviction, told me that there was only ever one microphone with Murray. They had worked out that if you had two, Murray would just talk over the top of you anyway, which is what happened all the way through his Formula 1 career, even with James Hunt, which is why they used to fall out so much. Murray had this lovely infectious style but he would get so enthralled with the race that he just wouldn't shut up and the other person couldn't get a word in. I found that the best way was to tug on his sleeve when I wanted to chip in or add some detail to what he was saying.

But there's no doubt that working with Murray was the broadcasting equivalent of being teammate to the World Champion. The man was just so good at what he did and I learned a lot from him, as well as some other great professionals at the Beeb on both sides of the camera – in particular I remember a director, a stern Scotsman, called Jim Reside. Jim was like a strict schoolteacher, so obviously Barry and I hated him, but he actually taught us a lot in terms of when to speak and when not and what terms might be inappropriate to use and so on. I remember Barry saying something like, 'He's from Dunfermline in Scotland', and Jim barking down the line in his thick Scottish accent saying: 'You wouldn't say Aylesbury in England would you?' His other big thing was to pull you up if you used a term like 'disaster' during a race commentary. 'It is *no* a disaster!' he would say. 'A disaster is when multiple people are killed.' These were, of course, all fair points and provided just the kind of BBC education that has shaped many broadcasters before and since.

For the last three or four years of my truck racing career,

any weekend that I wasn't racing I would be commentating, usually on British Superbikes with my great friend Barry Nutley. It was just my luck that, yet again, as one door closed another opened and thankfully for me the corridor was always short. I found commentating to be an interesting challenge and I enjoyed trying to describe what I was seeing in a reasonably erudite manner. Keeping my profile up was a big part of it too, I'll be honest. I always understood how important this was, so any television work was a great way of me staying in the public eye and maintaining a strong link to racing. I've always been good at talking myself out of things and entertaining people, so it seemed like a natural fit.

After dipping in and out of the job during the nineties with the likes of Nick, Murray and Barry, my first full season as a co-commentator came along in 2000, when the BBC took on World Superbikes. Once again Sheenie had been involved, convincing Mark Wilkin to team me up with this young Australian commentator he'd come across while working for Network Ten on their coverage of the V8 Supercars in Sydney.

Leigh Diffey – BBC World Superbike Commentator 2000–2001

The season started at Kyalami in South Africa and I pretty much kept my head down – I was new to the job and I was keen to impress, obviously. I had only just moved over to the UK from Australia but I found myself back there a few weeks later for round two of the World Superbike season at Phillip Island, sharing a room with Stavros in this stunning bed and breakfast overlooking Smiths Beach. The first morning we were due at the track I was up bright and early and spent ages ironing my new BBC shirt for the day. I jumped into the shower, leaving Steve still asleep in bed. When I came out, the bastard had my shirt on! I had to iron myself another one, and that was basically the start of life with the daftest, most selfish motherfucker I ever met! I remember later that year I was working for Channel 10 reporting on a car rally called the London to Sydney Marathon. It meant that straight after the World Superbike race at Hockenheim I had to leave and spend the next eleven days visiting ten different countries, before heading straight to Misano for the next World Superbike round. So, naively, I gave Stavros my BBC shirts and asked him if he'd do me the favour of getting them washed and pressed and take them to Misano for me. 'No problem mate,' he said, and packed the shirts in his bag. Sure enough we met up at Misano a couple of weeks later and he handed me three neatly pressed and folded shirts, which I gratefully took back to my room. But I was so fucking tired from all the travel I didn't even bother to hang them, I just went straight to bed. The next morning I slipped one of the shirts on and headed to the track. I kept getting funny looks and a few laughs from people and wondered what the fuck they were all looking at, when I bumped into some colleagues from Channel 10, who all burst into fits of giggles. That fucker had got his wife to iron the word 'STIFFY' in three-inch-high letters right across the back.

Stiffy was great fun, and even though he was indeed a little 'stiff' for those first few races we soon managed to loosen him up and he quickly became my partner in crime. I even gave him an advanced course in stage maroon engineering at Lausitzring one year, where we hijacked the birthday celebrations for the Honda team boss Neil Tuxworth by loading his cake with explosives and running a huge length of cable that I clipped from the circuit PA cable under the table and out of the side of the hospitality unit. Everybody was making a big deal about Neil's birthday and right at the point when they were all singing happy birthday and he was about to blow the candles out, we exploded the cake right in his face.

We had a few laughs during those early days but I have to say it wasn't always fun and games because there was actually a fair amount of animosity between us commentators and our glamorous new presenter Suzi Perry, who had arrived from Sky Sports. I guess it started because Stiffy was under the impression that he was going to be presenting, rather than just commentating, and frankly I was still something of a chauvinist. At the time I just couldn't see why a girl was presenting our sport. It's blatantly sexist, I know, but that was the world I had come from. Girls in motorsport, as far as I knew it, were for holding the umbrellas before the race and having fun with after.

But Suzi was a pioneer for female motorsport presenters and the real reason she was getting more attention than us was because she was a good-looking young girl with a lot going for her. I don't think Leigh or I liked that very much. But we came to respect her because she was very good at what she did. I remember sitting down with her at the NEC bike show and apologising because we did get off on the wrong foot and I recognised that I was out of order. After that we had our occasional differences, of course, but on the whole we spent many happy years working together. She is still a good friend to this day and remains one of the very best motorsport presenters in the game.

Having said that, I don't know if I really helped much to smooth things over between Stiffy and Suzi – especially when she brought one of these fancy new digital cameras to the racetrack. Most of us had never seen one before and Suzi was loving pointing the thing around, taking snaps of everybody. By the time Sunday evening came around we were all bloody sick of it, so when we went to the Castrol Honda hospitality unit for our traditional post-race beer I decided to take a few snapshots of my own. While Suzi had her back turned I pointed the camera at Stiffy and said: 'Smile!' Then I nipped off around the back of the truck and took another picture, this time straight down the front of my underpants. I came back and got Stiffy to pose for another mugshot, then dashed off and got another pic of my crown jewels. The idea was obviously to make Suzi think Stiffy was deliberately filling her camera with this filth, although it was just a bit of fun and I never did find out if the photos came out because I believe she gave the camera to her mum!

Anyway, Stiffy was the first commentator I properly worked with and it was a shame that it wasn't for longer because unfortunately he fell out with the BBC at the end of 2001 and picked up a great job over in the USA commentating on Formula 1. It's a role he still does now for NBC, where he is recognised as one of their top presenters and commentators, which is no surprise to me because to this day I rate him as one of the best I have ever worked with and I believe the BBC made a big mistake in letting him go.

As well as travelling to the World Superbike rounds we also did the British Superbikes and if we couldn't make the races because of a clash, we'd go down to the offices of a production company called BHP in Russell Square, and later to Octagon in Wimbledon, where I would often bump into Murray Walker doing the same thing for the touring cars, alongside a former driver called Charlie Cox. I used to ride my motorcycle down there and even though commuting clearly wasn't really my thing, I managed to make the job a little more interesting whenever I could – including one particular day when a few minutes into my journey I noticed a magpie caught in a trap.

These traps are everywhere in rural Hertfordshire because

magpies are such a pest – they raid other birds' nests and eat the eggs – but instead of letting this poor bird die there I thought it would be a nice thing for me to relocate it to an exciting new life in the big city. So I released the magpie from the trap, popped it into my backpack and jumped back on the bike. Once I got to the office, I unzipped my bag and nipped off to hide in the loos for a few minutes. Of course, by the time I came back the bird was causing absolute pandemonium. They had to evacuate the building and open all the windows and doors and eventually it flew out. A bit like me in the seventies, I like to think it lived a much more fun life in happening West London than it ever could have hoped for in boring old Steeple Morden.

After four years of covering World Superbikes, by 2004 the BBC had regained the live broadcast rights to what had now been rebranded as the MotoGP World Championship and I was like a pig in shit. I was back in the Grand Prix paddock on the cusp of a golden era for the sport, with the 500cc two-stroke machines of my era now an increasingly distant memory and a new generation of 990cc four-strokes taking over the world. At the centre of the sport's blossoming success was a young man by the name of Valentino Rossi, already a six-time World Champion and in some people's eyes already established as the G.O.A.T. – the Greatest of All Time.

After winning the last ever 500cc title in 2001 and the first two in MotoGP with the all-conquering Honda V5, in 2004 Rossi had achieved something almost unthinkable, proving his genius by switching manufacturers and presenting Yamaha with their first premier-class title in twelve years. With his ir-repressible charm and charisma off the track and killer instinct on it, Rossi was putting our sport back in the mainstream spotlight in a way that only my great friend Barry Sheene had previously managed. And even though Britain had not produced a Grand Prix winner since Sheenie's final victory at Anderstorp in Sweden, some 23 years earlier, the sport finally had another global superstar and naturally the BBC wanted a piece of the action.

I barely knew it at the time but it turned out that I had first met this remarkable young man many years earlier. In the early eighties I didn't have much time for my own children, so I was hardly likely to pay attention to somebody else's. As such, the little rugrat following my Italian friend and rival Graziano Rossi around the paddock didn't really register much in my mind and, obviously, nobody could have known then just what he would go on to become.

Like most of the younger racers at the time, Graziano idolised Barry and they always got on really well because Barry would speak to him in Italian, which of course I couldn't do. But I still really liked the guy and we were good mates. Probably the only thing I didn't like about Graziano was that all the girls in the paddock fancied him, including my girlfriend Linda! When he came out of his caravan she would run to the window to catch a glimpse of this Italian playboy with his long dark hair, fantastic beard and quirky style. I raced against him a lot during that era and although he wasn't the fastest – I'd say I probably beat him more times than he beat me – he certainly had a natural talent and flair for racing that he passed on to his young boy.

The admiration Graziano had for Barry was also inherited by Valentino, who grew up in the paddock and was always a great student of the sport. Just a few months after Barry's death in 2003, Valentino paid a wonderful tribute to him, flying a huge number 7 flag on the cool-down lap of his victory in the Australian Grand Prix at Phillip Island. In many ways Sheene and Rossi are kindred spirits; flamboyant mavericks with more than a touch of genius and an aptitude for marketing themselves like nobody before or since. Indeed, Valentino had been the first World Champion since Barry to forgo the fabled number 1 and keep his own number, 46, which has now become a hugely recognisable global brand.

There were other signs of Barry's influence on the young Valentino Rossi, most notably his Australian crew at HRC headed by Jeremy Burgess, who had previously worked with Mick Doohan, another Sheene protégé. Mick had been forced to retire through injury in 1999 and even though I'm sure the Japanese at HRC were keen to keep those boys together when they signed this Italian wonderkid in 2000, I have equally little doubt that Barry will have pushed open a few doors and helped the whole thing to happen. Barry was doing quite a bit of work at the races for Australian television at the time, so you can just bet he will have been at the back of Valentino's garage, telling him which tyre to use and everything else, as he did to us all.

I don't think it's any surprise that Barry was as much of a hero to Valentino, and an influence on him, as he was to the rest of us, so for me it was quite nice that when I returned to the Grand Prix paddock as a commentator with the BBC in 2004, my first task was to ride his title-winning Yamaha after the final round of that historic season at Valencia. Almost exactly twenty years after parking my OW53 against the pit wall at Silverstone, here I was about to throw my fifty-year-old leg over the factory YZR-M1 that just 24 hours earlier the newly-crowned World Champion had guided to victory in front of 120,000 screaming fans in the Valencian Grand Prix.

I had spent weeks worrying about the occasion, making sure I was fit and sharp. I had researched the bike, how Rossi rode it and what made it tick. Thankfully the conditions were perfect and it was on a crisp and clear October morning that I stood there in my underpants, looking at my leathers and feeling every bit as nervous as I had ever been before the start of a race during my own career. In thirty minutes' time I would be straddling the most beautiful motorcycle in the world, if only for a couple of laps. It would be like speed-dating a supermodel, although at least I was guaranteed a ride. It would be the ride of my life. 'How long will I last?' 'How will she respond when I open her up?' These nagging doubts were all too familiar to me.

My heart was pounding but the sheer excitement I felt inside was in stark contrast to the sheer boredom on the faces of the Yamaha mechanics, stuck at the circuit for another day at the end of a long season, just so a bunch of journalists and has-beens could ride the motorcycle they had turned into the best in the world, most of them with no appreciation for just how good it really was. Even I knew, quite frankly, that anybody who is unable to get to within five seconds of the circuit record is not qualified to have an opinion on a MotoGP bike, and that included me. However, setting off down the pit-lane I made a big effort to at least look the part, standing up on the foot pegs and pulling my leathers out of my arse – just like the great man himself. Imagine if I had fallen off then!

It is virtually impossible to describe what riding one of these incredibly exotic and expensive machines is like, as very few people have experienced anything even remotely similar. And since very few of us have had a blow job from Kate Moss, let's use the supermodel analogy again and imagine that it's probably a bit like that: it feels fantastic, it's all over too quickly, and the best bit by far is telling your mates that you've done it.

Seriously, the most relevant comparison I can make for anybody who rides a road-going superbike like a Yamaha R1 or a Suzuki GSX-R or a Honda Fireblade is for them to imagine how focusing those things are in first or second gear. Well, a MotoGP bike pulls exactly the same in fifth and sixth! The thing wants to rip your arms out of their sockets in every gear and then one little finger on those carbon brakes and the bike is standing on its nose. At least that slots your shoulders back into place!

Whenever I have ridden one of these incredible machines I am always aware, first of all, of how privileged I am. But I am also very conscious of not making myself look like a twat. So there has to be a compromise between concentrating on the job in hand, pushing the bike as fast as I dare, arse nibbling the seat the whole way round, or dawdling around trying to think of what I will say to the camera when the fun stops. Being a bloke, I am no good at multitasking and considering the consequences should something go wrong, I decided to concentrate on having fun.

Thankfully I managed to keep it upright and survive that weekend in Valencia, which was a blessing – not because I had spent the afternoon riding the fastest motorcycle in the world, but because of an incident in a tapas bar later that evening that proved to be far, far more dangerous.

13

Chairman Mouse

A key piece of equipment in the box of tricks that I take every-where with me is a home-made contraption fashioned from a note-snatcher, which is basically a fishing line on a spring recoil with a twenty-pound note on the end. Just as somebody goes to pick the note up off the floor, you press a button that retracts it; it's a joke shop classic. However, mine is a bit more special than that because it occurred to me one day that replac-ing the twenty-pound note with a furry little toy mouse that I bought from a pet shop has the potential to wreak much more havoc.

I've had some great fun with it over the years, making waitresses drop piles of plates and just generally scaring the shit out of friends and fellow diners in restaurants. So when I walked past a couple gazing romantically into each other's eyes in a tapas bar on that fateful evening in Valencia, it was another opportunity that was too good to miss.

We were on a typical BBC night out with the whole team of around sixteen people, including me, Charlie Cox and Suzi Perry. I'd been working with Charlie since Stiffy had gone off to the States and I struck up an equally close partnership with him. Like Stiffy he was a sharp-witted Australian, although I have to say he has the broadest vocabulary of anybody I've ever met, allied to a sharp business mind, and particularly after a few glasses of wine he is an exceptional raconteur who makes great company.

This particular evening had started, as usual, in the hotel bar and after a few beers we headed into town and located the tapas bar somebody had been recommended, where we eventually tucked into a few morsels to eat alongside several bottles of Rioja. As the wine flowed, so the evening livened up, and after draining another glass of vino I decided now was a good time to cause a bit of havoc.

Making my way to the bathroom and scanning the restaurant for a victim, I clocked these two star-crossed lovers whispering sweet nothings across the table. 'Perfecto,' I thought, and pulling the mouse from my pocket as I sidled past their table I casually flicked it with the accuracy that only years of practice can hone, right into the middle of their paella. No sooner had it touched down than I pressed the recoil switch, sending my little furry mouse scurrying through the rice, inadvertently picking up a prawn that got tangled on the line, for extra shock effect.

To my surprise it was the bloke who screamed first, jumping up onto his chair as the mouse shot back towards me, dragging the innocent prawn as hostage and sending a full bottle of wine crashing over in the commotion as the waiters came running to the table to see what the problem was. I sensed my toilet break was now an opportune excuse to make a swift exit so I dashed off to the loo before I burst out laughing and blew my cover. I waited in the toilets for a little while until I figured things had calmed down and then casually made my way back towards the BBC table, wearing the fake 'Billy Bob' teeth that I always keep in my pocket as my only disguise.

Just as I was about to sit down and find out the delicious details of what had gone on while I was in temporary hiding, this

Spanish Romeo appeared out of nowhere and came straight for me with his steak knife! Clearly I had interrupted a moment of intense passion – I must have ruined his shag because I can't imagine what else could make a man so bloody angry! I desperately grabbed for my chair and just managed to get it up in time to hold off his first lunge, but the lunatic kept coming, trying to stab me. It took a bunch of waiters to intervene and disarm the crazy bastard before dragging him to the door and throwing him out! At least the rest of my table were entertained, with some bright spark nicknaming me 'Chairman Mouse', but I must admit I was glad to get out of that restaurant and back to the relative safety of a racetrack.

Suzi Perry – BBC World Superbike and MotoGP Presenter 2000–2009

The thing about Steve is that he never seems to quite recognise when a practical joke has gone too far, and that evening in Valencia was a great example. I remember him holding this madman off with a chair and looking at me desperately saying: 'You speak some Spanish! Tell him I was joking!' All this with his stupid fake teeth still in. He just can't tell when the atmosphere has changed from funny to seriously uncomfortable. He is uncontrollable. I don't know anybody else like that. But then that is all part of his charm. Travelling the world with MotoGP is a dream job but anybody who travels a lot for work knows how tough it can be too, so having somebody like Steve along is a treat because he keeps you laughing. Even though his jokes are always the same, like the bloody fart machine or the fake dog poo, different cultures react differently and watching him getting into trouble and then trying to worm his way out of it was all part of the entertainment. I remember being in an airport lounge in Japan

People always accused me of living my life in Barry Sheene's slipstream. Believe me, it was a hell of a place to be.

I got fired by Suzuki at the end of 1977 but was thrown a lifeline by George Harrison, who was a huge fan of the racing and used to come and hang out with us and other celebrities like Eric Idle.

With a generous gift from George and some added sponsorship from Makaha skateboards, I was back racing and earning more money than I had as a factory rider. (LAT)

A 'player-manager' before the term had been invented, I ran a Yamaha in the British Superstock Championship in 1986 with sponsorship from Loctite and signed Kenny Irons to run as my team-mate. Kenny won the title and was as big a talent as Niall Mackenzie or Carl Fogarty, in my opinion. I was devastated when he left to join Heron Suzuki in 1987, and even more so the following season when he died in a collision with one of my riders.

Loctite's Managing Director Geoff Bennett was the butt of one of my most favourite practical jokes, although surprisingly this wasn't it: signing Keith Heuwen and Trevor Nation to ride for us in 1987.

Easily my best signing as Team Manager was Terry Rymer. He had a cracking year for us in 1989, bringing the British Superstock Championship back to the team, while also becoming the first-ever British rider to win a World Superbike event with a superb ride at Manfeild in New Zealand.

Racing trucks started off as a bit of a laugh, but I ended up signing a factory contract with Mercedes worth more than anything I rode for as a motorcycle racer, and won five World titles. (BP)

Truck racing became a big deal for the manufacturers and a huge rivalry developed between Mercedes and MAN. After a bruising race in Nürburgring in 1991, the big boss at Mercedes, Helmut Werner, was able to present me with the winner's trophy.

With my first full-time commentary partner Leigh Diffey and World Superbike Champion Carl Fogarty ahead of the 2000 season. I loved the challenge of trying to describe the action on screen and as a partner 'Stiffy' was one of the best I ever worked with.

Riding Valentino Rossi's Yamaha YZR-M1 at Valencia in 2004 was a bit like a blow job from a supermodel: over too quickly but at least I could tell my mates it had happened!

Charlie Cox was my commentary-box buddy and partner-in-crime for a full decade. As a former British Touring Car Championship racer, he was the perfect hire car co-driver, and it was unusual for us to bring one back in one piece.

With Charlie, Matt Roberts and the rest of the BBC crew after they had all helped me dig my hire car out of a ditch on a dirt road between the hotel and the track at Mugello . . .

My own personal airline, Plummet Airways, getting ready for another questionable take-off.

'Revenge is a dish best served cold.' My mate Dave Morris pranked me with this stag's head in my bed.

'Do ya wanna bet on it?' With Jet from Gladiators and some toff on a polo horse, which I raced in my Mercedes sports car on the television show *You Bet*. As usual, I found an unconventional way to win. (LWT)

As an avid self-preservationist, the Isle of Man TT was not a race I excelled in, but I did manage a podium in 1985, only to be disqualified subsequently for running an illegal fuel tank. It was an innocent mistake.

I am glad I raced at the TT, if only because I can now commentate on it with some understanding of what the riders are going through. I also get to spend time with a great team at North One TV, including my on-screen pals Craig Doyle, James Whitham and Steve Plater.

My last-ever professional motorcycle race was at Macau in 1986. Officially I was banned from the country due to my explosive behaviour the year before.

Team BBC. (Watts Where Media)

Charlie's Angel and me.
(Watts Where Media)

Despite their 'unusual'
childhood, which included
holidays to Great Yarmouth
in an ambulance to avoid the
traffic, my kids Joe and Frankie
have turned out pretty well!

My wife Michelle is the love of
my life and she helps keep me
smiling pretty much all the
time, often at her own expense!
Bless her.

and he hid the fart machine behind the breakfast cereals. There was something quite extraordinary about the way Japanese people reacted to the noises it made. Of course, we were all bursting with laughter but eventually somebody came and confiscated it. Steve was apoplectic, begging this member of staff to get his beloved fart machine back. It was rare to see him lose his sense of humour, although there is one occasion that really sticks in my mind, when he was driving a hire car back from Jerez to Seville with Charlie Cox and me. Whenever you went in a car with those two you were taking your life into your hands – whether it was driving across a live army training ground in Laguna Seca or trying to do doughnuts and getting stuck in a cornfield in Germany, we never took a car back that wasn't damaged. Anyway, Charlie and I used to sing a lot in the car, which Steve hated, so we were winding him up singing along to 'Mandy' by Barry Manilow, but we changed the words to 'Stevie' because that's what somebody had called him that weekend. Steve put his ear plugs in and wrapped a jumper or something around his head to block out the racket, but we kept on. Eventually he just stopped the car on the motorway, got out and walked off. We were laughing hysterically at the sight of him wandering down the central reservation with his ear plugs in and this jumper wrapped around his head. The man lives completely in his own world.

Over the years I have been lucky enough to ride some of the most exotic motorcycles and drive some of the most expensive cars on the planet. However, I have to say that the one piece of equipment that has given me the most pleasure in life is my fart machine. Ever since I started importing them from America back in the eighties I have always had one to hand and it never fails to get a laugh, at least from me, no matter how inappropriate the occasion. In fact, I often find the most inappropriate occasions are the best: a royal engagement, for example, or under oath in a court of law.

In the months after Barry's death there were a lot of memorial events in his honour, including a plaque unveiling during the Scarborough Gold Cup weekend at Oliver's Mount by Prince Philip, Duke of Edinburgh. The weekend coincided with the centenary of the Auto-Cycle Union, so all the big cheeses of British motorcycling were there too. These royal engagements are organised with military precision and, according to the schedule, His Royal Highness would be escorted over to us by a group of bodyguards at eleven o'clock on the dot. There was a group of us there – me, Phil Read, Mick Grant, Jamie Whitham and a few others – and at precisely 11.02 a.m. he came over to shake our hands, starting with Readie, who as an MBE took priority. Unbeknownst to Readie, or anybody else, I had managed to hide my fart machine under the tank on his bike and as soon as the Prince put his hand out, I let it rip with the first of five varieties of bottom hair harmonies. Whit and I almost pissed ourselves as the Duke's two bodyguards looked at each other as if to say, 'Oh no, not again!' while poor old Readie can't have been sure that he hadn't blown a bum note himself!

While that one played out very much in the open air, the elaborate, carved wooden benches of Lancaster Court provided much better acoustics when I stopped off there on the way back home from the Isle of Man to act as the expert witness in a case. Unusually, as we were en route, Michelle was with me so she was sitting up in the gallery as I took my place in the witness box. By now we had been together for ten years so she was well-versed in my childish ways, especially the fart machine, but even she remains susceptible to an unexpected embarrassment.

There were around fifteen to twenty other people there – solicitors, clerks of the court, counsel and the rest – but Michelle was sitting on her own, minding her own business and reading a book while she waited for me to give evidence. Unbeknownst to her, my fart machine was in her handbag and my remote control was in my pocket. And as soon as I had sworn to tell the truth, the whole truth and nothing but the truth, I hit the button. With that, a bottom blast befitting a bitter-drinking bricklayer echoed around the gallery, prompting the whole court – judge included – to glare up in Michelle's direction. The poor girl grabbed her bag and her book and went running for the door, everybody making the obvious assumption that she was dashing straight for the toilet! That, I must say, was one of my best ever hits.

As Suzi mentioned, the fart machine got me in plenty of trouble while working for the BBC although I managed to cause an even bigger stink at the Day of Champions annual fundraiser, held on the Thursday before the British Grand Prix, in aid of a wonderful charity called Riders for Health, which has since been renamed Two Wheels for Life. There are various events throughout the Day of Champions, with a live stage show, stuntmen, photographic opportunities with the superstars of the MotoGP paddock and a huge memorabilia auction. One of the main events at the Donington Park event in 2009 was a lap of the track on board a National Express coach, with one of the top riders taking the microphone to give a guided tour.

It had got to about 4 p.m. and the day was coming steadily to a close when I was approached by my old friend Andrea Coleman, whom I have known since the seventies as she was married to my teammate Tom Herron when he was killed in 1978. Andrea has stayed involved in motorcycling ever since that tragic day and now does a wonderful job running the charity alongside her husband Barry.

Anyway, she came up to me and said that all the current riders were now occupied with team meetings and such, and could I do her a favour and take hold of the microphone for a final bus tour? I thought: 'I can do better than that!' So I gathered a BBC film crew together and we all got on the bus with the punters. The poor driver, who'd been doing 25mph laps of Donington Park all day, looked bored to hell. 'You look like you've had a long day, mate,' I said to him. 'You go and have a cup of tea. Give me the keys – I can drive this thing.'

The driver turned to a couple of the passengers as if to say, 'Is he telling the truth?' and they were like: 'Come on, he's a truck racing World Champion!'

'Okay, but whatever you do don't go over fifty-five miles an hour, because I'll get fired,' he said, as he clambered wearily down the steps.

'Trust me,' I called after him. 'I'm a doctor!'

A few moments later we were hurtling towards Redgate corner, the first turn on the circuit, where all of these punters would have been expecting me to slow down and give them some information on how fast the MotoGP bikes would be going through there, what gear they would be in and everything else. Instead, I said: 'Here we go into Redgate corner . . . and we're going way too fast so if you don't all jump over to the right side of the bus immediately we're going to tip over!' So they all jumped to the right of the bus. The problem is that the next section of track is Craner Curves, which is a quick switchback of left and rights that caused more than a bit of confusion. I had a bit of understeer going on and the thing was sliding about all over the place, causing the lads who were busy hanging the advertising boards around the outside of the track a little consternation. By lap three they had all jumped over to the other side of the tyre walls, although they needn't have worried because we were getting the hang of it.

The passengers were having a great time and they cheered wildly when we hit 90mph down the straight. It seemed the officials weren't as impressed because at the start of lap four they pulled me in, which was a shame because I think I could have gone even faster. Still, I was pretty pleased with my 2:58 lap in the wet conditions and, as far as I'm aware, that still stands to this day as the lap record for a National Express coach at Donington Park.

That evening I was back in my hotel room, enjoying some room service before an early night ahead of what was going to be a busy and important weekend, when I got a phone call from Keith Huewen, who had stayed late at the track to help out during the auction.

'Stavros, was that you driving that bloody bus around the track today?'

'Yes,' I replied.

'Well if I was you I'd keep my head down because I'm standing in the press room right now looking out of the window and there are three or four members of Race Direction out there overseeing a full track clean-up operation.'

It turned out that in attempting to work out what some mystery fluid was that had appeared on the circuit on the eve of the British Grand Prix, Stuart Higgs, who is the British Superbike Race Director and an FIM Steward at several MotoGP events, the Course Director and Paul Butler, who was Race Director for MotoGP, had been doing the old engineer's trick of tasting a little bit of the offending fluid off the end of their fingers to see if it was water, coolant or oil. Of course, it was no such thing. In fact, we'd managed to get the bus on such an angle that all of the piss and shit had run out of the toilet on the bus and leaked onto the track! The next morning Stuart called me a very nasty name but I'm pleased to say I have forgiven him for that and we are good friends again.

I thought the whole episode had passed when, a few days after footage of our record-breaking lap had aired as part of the BBC's coverage of the Grand Prix, I had a phone call from a representative of National Express. This gentleman had been given my number by my producer Belinda, who dropped me like a hot stone when she received an official complaint about the unauthorised and reckless use of a National Express coach on national television. He didn't react too well when I suggested he introduce passenger involvement to his services as standard but eventually I appeased him by explaining that, of course, we had concocted the whole thing using the magic of television and at no point had the passengers on board been in any danger.

So far that remains my one and only flirtation with bus racing but I hope it's not the last because I think it has huge potential as a winter motorsport that could fill all of those empty dates in the calendar. Just think about it! Instead of the fans turning up to Brands Hatch and sitting on the bankings under their umbrellas in the cold and the rain, they could all be sitting aboard the vehicle with the driver! They'd get live on-board coverage of the race – we could even commentate it for them – and they'd get to share in the success of the winner. I would even introduce a handicap system so that at the end of each lap the bus in the lead has to send two more passengers upstairs. I can't see any possible reason why it would fail.

That same weekend at the British Grand Prix, some bright spark on the BBC team thought it would make an amusing introduction to the show if Charlie and I arrived in a motorcycle and sidecar, accompanied by the theme tune to *Wallace and Gromit*. I was bang up for it, but unsurprisingly Charlie wasn't so keen, especially because he was going to have to play the role of Gromit. He could be a grumpy old sod at the best of times so he fitted the role perfectly, and when we came in after two laps of Donington Park with me tipping him two feet off the ground through the corners he had no problems getting into character when the production assistant said: 'Try to look annoyed, Charlie!' If you saw that piece when it aired on BBC2 on the Sunday, I can tell you that every bit of his pissed-off expression was genuine.

Charlie and I had a great relationship, although he made it clear from very early on that as much as he loved watching me playing pranks on other people, as far as he was concerned he was off limits. So I did try my best to resist but occasionally opportunities presented themselves that I just couldn't pass up. And they never failed to piss him right off.

One of them concerned this leather satchel he had, which had been given to him as a freebie by the clothing company Gas at some Honda event about ten years previously. Over the years he had become strangely attached to the bag, which he called 'Brownie', even though by now it was in a complete state, all battered and held together with duct tape and safety pins. I don't know why he didn't just get a new one, because Charlie is not short of a few quid, but for some reason he loved this bag and at the start of every season it would make another appearance.

Suzi and I used to nag him about it all the time – he looked like some kind of vagrant wandering around the airports with this tatty old bag – so eventually we decided to take matters into our own hands. Coming back from a race at Mugello we had all packed our luggage into the boot of the hire car for the journey to Bologna airport, but I got out and made out I had forgotten something in my suitcase. Once out of sight around the back of the car, I emptied out any paperwork and all the other crap he'd accumulated and hooked the strap onto the boot catch, leaving 'Brownie' trailing behind the car on the road. By the time we got to the airport there was hardly anything left on the end of the strap and Suzi and I were just pissing ourselves laughing. Meanwhile Charlie, without saying a word to either of us, collected Brownie's tattered remains and put them carefully into a nearby bin. The weirdest thing was that he then spent a couple of minutes peering in, like he was saying goodbye. He was so upset he literally wouldn't talk to me for about two days.

As well as being averse to practical jokes, Charlie is also allergic to fish and he'd given me plenty of warnings not to get up to any trouble with anything to do with our scaly friends. However, one evening we were out with the whole BBC team, having a few drinks over dinner, and with a little encouragement I agreed it was time to stitch Charlie up. It was decided that this huge fish skeleton that had been left on somebody's plate was the ideal prop, so with Charlie holding court at the other end of the table I discreetly wrapped it up in a napkin and took it back to the hotel. The plan was that I would drop it on the desk in the commentary box while we were live on air the next day and say a code word so that everybody back in the gallery would know when it had happened. After a few laps of the race, just as Charlie was digging around in his bag for half a Mars bar or something to nibble on, which he always liked to do during a broadcast, I dropped the skeleton on the desk and shouted: 'Wow! Look at that! He's fishtailing into the corner!' As the whole gallery burst into laughter in our ears, Charlie took one look at the fish bones, stood up, removed his headphones and just walked out of the commentary booth, leaving me to commentate on my own! He came back after a little while but he was not at all impressed.

When he wasn't upset with me Charlie was great fun, a really smart guy with scant regard for authority, and we had a genuine friendship that continues to this day. In some ways he is a typically blunt Australian, who to my enduring delight took the famous Aussie 'Do I Look Like I Give a Fuck?' attitude to whole new heights at Indianapolis in 2008, when the MotoGP race was red-flagged due to the untimely arrival of Hurricane Ike after just eight laps. This was bad news for Charlie because he was due on a flight out of Indianapolis to Los Angeles, where he had a connection to Sydney for some important business meetings he had down there. If he missed the connection at LAX the whole trip would be ruined and he was cutting it fine as it was.

Anticipating that the traffic would be heavy outside the circuit after the race, he'd arranged through a friend for some bloke to pick him up on a motorcycle and whisk him to the airport to make sure he got there on time. So, while Race Direction were taking their time deciding whether they could restart the race or if they would be forced to postpone it, and the BBC2 schedulers were panicking over whether they could extend our on-air time and drop *Antiques Roadshow* or whatever shite they had lined up after us, Charlie went into full default 'DILLIGAF' mode.

Meanwhile, down in the pit-lane, Suzi and our reporter Matt Roberts were running around trying to grab people for interviews to keep us on air, but they were rapidly running out of subjects as the teams slammed shut the garages and the whole circuit quite literally battened down the hatches. The storm had started to rip advertising hoardings from the perimeter fencing and blow them down the middle of the track and the amount of rain that was hammering down was creating huge puddles of standing water in every corner.

However, the scenes outside were nothing compared to the complete chaos that was going on in the commentary booth, where Belinda had a telephone in each hand – on one to Television Centre, trying frantically to buy us some more airtime, and on the other one trying to get a decision from Race Control about whether we would have a restart. Meanwhile, she was throwing incredulous looks at Charlie, who to her complete horror was now stripped off down to his underpants. He'd decided he wasn't hanging around to see what happened and there was no way he was getting his clothes wet on the back of that motorbike, so he was changing into the only alternative he had – a set of freebie British Airways First Class pyjamas!

He looked absolutely preposterous. I could barely hold myself together as I continued trying to talk sensibly over whatever pictures were on screen. But with no decision forthcoming from Race Direction, and despite Belinda's strongest protestations, Charlie just picked up his suitcase and strode out into the storm. I never got to see what he looked like on the back of that bike, so I can only imagine how the residents of Indianapolis might have reacted to the sight of a bloke on the back of a Harley in the pissing rain, clutching his belongings in nothing but his jim-jams and a crash helmet. And God only knows what they made of him when he arrived at the airport check-in, soaked to his skin, as he handed over his business class ticket to Australia.

Charlie really was my partner in crime and, as a former racer himself, my perfect hire car co-driver for a whole decade. We caused havoc on the roads from Monza to Motegi and whereas most people I gave lifts to would be screaming for me to slow down, Charlie would be checking the coast was clear for overtakes. In fact, I would argue it is mainly Charlie's fault that I am now blacklisted by all but a couple of rental companies, because we crashed or bent so many of their vehicles over the years.

Charlie Cox – BBC World Superbike and MotoGP Commentator 2003–2013

Notwithstanding the very rich, purposeful way we used to get to the airport from the track in Qatar, when he took it upon himself to use a black marker pen to alter the Arabic letters on the number plate and thus go flat out through the numerous speed cameras en route, I think my best hire car tales with Stavros come from Italy. One of the most spectacular bits of road we ever came across on our travels was a dirt track between the Mugello circuit and the golf club where we stayed for the Italian MotoGP. The only time I ever weed myself laughing was on one of the only foolish occasions they gave us two cars and I gave him a little 'love tap' from behind going down the hill in a Fiat Panda. It launched him down the hill and he was bouncing so hard I could see air under the tyres at the back. The silly old bastard still didn't lift off the pedal. Every year there was an incident and in 2013 he parked it in a ditch for three days until we could get enough crew members together to help pull it out – and I still burned the clutch out on one of the other renters, trying to tow the damn thing! But the best one was very early on in our career together, covering World Superbikes at Monza. The town of Monza has these really wide bicycle lanes, completely separate from the road, almost wide enough for a car. The traffic was jammed, we were late and Suzi was sitting in the back getting all worked up. So next thing Stavros is driving down these cycle lanes, until they eventually diverted away from the road and through a park! There were people out cycling and running, families sitting eating picnics, couples playing Frisbee, all diving out of the way. It was like a scene from *The Sound of Music*, with this fucking car bouncing up and down the rolling hills and past the flower beds! We get to the other end and there was a copper at the gate guiding thousands of pedestrians into the circuit. She looked at us blankly, she just couldn't process the information. She obviously didn't have a form for this one, so she just let us through. It was remarkable. That was also the first car we had with a reversing camera. So on the way back from the circuit to the hotel that evening Stavros came up with this top plan to drive backwards through Monza using the reversing camera. He was doing really well, filtering, changing lanes and all the rest of it, flat out on the rev limiter, when this old dear behind looked at us, realised we were facing her and thought she was the one driving the wrong way. So she promptly threw a sudden U-turn and almost cleaned out our cameraman in the next car behind her! Meanwhile we made it all the way back to the hotel and hardly hit anything at all.

While some of the cars didn't make it back to the rental companies in one piece, some of them didn't make it back at all – like one of the shitty Protons we were always given in Malaysia. Leaving Sepang on the evening after the race the traffic was absolutely horrendous for what was only a couple of miles' drive to the airport. Charlie and I had an overnight flight to catch and with the roads completely gridlocked with race traffic we were certain to miss it unless I took drastic action. So I drove onto the grass verge and put my foot down, flying past all these poor buggers stuck in the jam.

The job was going an absolute dream until I heard something scrape on the underside of the car. Suddenly the fuel gauge started to drop quicker than a bride's knickers and the car ground to a halt. I'd driven straight over the top of an old road sign, which had been sheared to about ten inches high in a previous incident, and put a big slice straight through the fuel tank. There was no way that was getting fixed at the side of the road, so we left the keys in the car, rang the hire company and informed them it had run out of fuel and told them where it was. Then we managed to flag down a lift and made it to the airport with minutes to spare.

Colin Edwards – World Superbike Champion 2000 and 2002

After a race at Lausitzring my wife Aly and I were leaving the motorhome at the circuit and needed a lift to Berlin airport. Knowing Stavros and Charlie travelled together, and had an empty back seat, we got a plan together on the Sunday evening. 'Okay mate, me and Charlie will pick you two up at eight a.m. tomorrow.'

'All good, see ya then!!'

Well, 8 a.m. came and we are waiting . . . and waiting . . . At maybe 8.15 or 8.30 they come rollin' in hot. They both jumped out of the car in a half panic, making no sense: 'Holy shit! Fucking hell! Big jump . . . rallycross . . . oil pan . . . shit!!' That's about 99.9 per cent accurate how the conversation went. Anyways, the reality was Stavros just had to hit his little rallycross section one more time in the rental car before heading home. And we all know what 'Just one more time!' means to Stavros. The car was pouring with smoke and there were bits hanging off it, dragging on the ground. In the end, it became clear this car wasn't going anywhere, so we all piled in the TV crew van instead. Unfortunately for Stavros we were one seat short, so he volunteered to serve his time riding in the back with the luggage. And of course he had his redneck 'Billy Bob' fake gnashers in, smiling at everyone on the way. Thankfully we all made it to our destination on time, with another new Stavros story to tell.

When we got to the airport I went up to the hire car desk with the keys and said: 'I'm afraid the car is not here as I attempted to drive it to the airport this morning and the oil light started flickering, so I decided the best course of action was to switch the ignition off and leave the car where it was.'

'That is very sensible,' replied the nice gentleman on the desk. 'You wouldn't believe how many cars we have destroyed by people who continue to drive them after the warning lights have come on.'

'Well, it's the least I can do,' I offered, informing him exactly where the car was before dashing off gleefully to catch my flight.

The guy couldn't have been more grateful – he even gave me a discount voucher off my next rental in exchange for my 'good deed' – but two weeks later the shit hit the fan when the BBC got a bill through the post for 12,500 euros! They chased me for months for the money but I got a witness to write a letter saying there was some debris that came off a lorry in front of us that must have got caught under the car or something like that. They must have known it was bollocks because the whole bottom of the car was written off, but I just refused to pay and eventually the whole thing went away.

Thankfully, I got away with that one, but if you do ever get into a similar situation here's a little tip: loosen the wheel nuts and drive it until the wheel comes off. Then you can simply blame the whole accident on poor maintenance! That old trick that I perfected on Mr Caruthers' car back in 1966 has got me out of many a sticky situation since. So who says I didn't learn anything at school?

14

Man alive!

My first experience of motorcycle racing on the Isle of Man was in 1972, when I travelled over with the Pourus Racing boys from the Coach and Horses to watch the world-famous TT from the kerbside. I was on my Triumph, a couple of the lads were on Velocettes and somebody else had a Norton. Each bike was a bigger pile of junk than the next and between us we probably broke down every twenty miles, but we were laughing all the way. As usual, I took a bag of tricks with me to keep us entertained, including a few sachets of laxatives, which I emptied into the milk jug at Mrs Miggins' bedsit in Douglas. Everybody who ate breakfast that morning, which included quite a large party of German tourists, had the shits for two days. It literally wiped the place out.

With no Isle of Man TT coverage on the television, all we knew about the races was what we had read in magazines or been told in the pub, so you can imagine how blown away we were when we saw them for the first time in the flesh. It actually rained for much of that weekend and I can remember getting wet sitting under the trees at Braddan Bridge and hearing on the portable radio that the championship leader Gilberto Parlotti had disappeared over the edge of the Verandah – a series of fast right-hand corners up on the mountain section with a steep drop off the edge of the road into the fields below – and died. Parlotti was a great mate of Giacomo Agostini and it was partly down to this that Ago stopped doing the TT. For me it was the first time I had heard of a guy dying in a motorcycle race, but nobody around us seemed that bothered because apparently it was a regular occurrence there.

Three years later I returned to the island to compete in the Manx Grand Prix on Harold Coppock's TZ350, accompanied this time by my mechanic, Martin Brookman. I couldn't have been more excited; I had spent my whole life with people telling me to be careful, to slow down, and being chased by the police and told off for speeding, yet here the advice was the complete opposite. 'It's a public road but you have to ride as fast as you possibly can.' It's crazy, really.

It was impossible to learn the whole 37¾-mile lap in one go, so we tried to do it in sections. We drove five miles up the road and then, to make sure I didn't get confused, I sat in the back of the van while Martin drove back and then repeated the same five miles over and over again: from the start to Ballacraine, Ballacraine to Ballaugh, Ballaugh to Ramsey and then over the Mountain, making sure I was happy with each section before moving on to the next. It was such a long way round, we genuinely had to work out if we could afford the fuel for another lap.

Of course, there were no on-board videos to look at on YouTube, no games consoles, no invitation from the organisers to take a hire car around the circuit with Milky Quayle, the resident expert, like they have nowadays. Not that I'm saying it's really any easier to learn now, because believe me the first time you actually ride a lap of the TT course it is like nothing else you could ever experience anywhere – computer games or not!

Seeing it in a van at 30mph had been one thing, but trying to compute everything at three, four or even five times that speed was truly the most extraordinary thing ever. There were straw bales dotted around but the chances of hitting one were negligible. I heard stories of somebody crashing through the pub door at Ballacraine and there are countless corners named after people who didn't get through them, as well as these little additional memorials all around the track. I had been club racing for a couple of years in the UK without considering it but I didn't need too many laps of the TT course before it entered my head that this sport could kill me. I remember seeing a lady through the window of her front room and thinking: 'If I crash here I could end up in there!'

However, day by day, session by session, these ridiculous speeds on open roads become the norm. You get drunk on the sheer speed, you become acclimatised to it, and a bike that felt unrideable on day one somehow becomes rideable after two weeks. When I'm at the TT now I see guys who change everything on the bike over the course of a fortnight and then end up going back to whatever they had on the first day.

I can remember going back from the TT to somewhere like Mallory Park or Brands Hatch and I couldn't believe how much slower it felt. I know that a few guys like Mick Grant and John Williams, both TT specialists, always got better at short circuits after the event, and even though that was never the case for me, I did get used to travelling at such high speeds for such a long time and even now I can be driving along at 100mph and feel like I'm hardly moving.

However, I have never had a great memory and even at the end of my TT career I never really felt as if I knew the place properly. It is a part of what held me back. I was beaten by guys who focus all year on that one event. They spent months preparing for it, doing everything they could to give themselves even a tiny advantage, whereas I just wanted to get back home in one piece – never more so than on that first visit in 1975, when the engine on my Yamaha seized up during practice.

It wasn't an uncommon thing at the TT, especially at the Highlander pub, where it happened to me. You could go into the Highlander and half your mates would be there having a coffee because the same thing had happened to them. It was just after the fastest section of the circuit, flat out for three miles, before you shut the throttle into Greeba Castle. It happened most often during the early morning practice sessions when it was cool and the air was thick, so everybody had their bikes running lean and susceptible to a seizure.

When an engine seized on an old bike like that the pistons, which were made of alloy, would stick to the chromium-plated cylinders. Really the pistons were probably wrecked but if you couldn't afford new ones there was an old trick of removing the excess aluminium from the cylinder with caustic soda, which you could buy from a chemist. So Martin and I took the engine back to Mrs Miggins' bedsit, hoisted it up onto the bedroom table, took the cylinders off and got to work. Somehow, while Martin was busy working his magic on the engine, I managed to knock over the caustic soda and burn a hole in the carpet about six inches across.

I started panicking that Mrs Miggins would have the shits with me for the second time, so in the dead of night, once we had got the engine all fixed up, we quietly took all the furniture out of the room and placed it gently on the landing. We had worked out that the room was shaped in an almost perfect square, so we lifted the carpet up at each corner and swivelled it around ninety degrees so that the burned patch was now underneath the bed. I was so pleased with our little scam that I must have told everybody in the paddock, including a reporter from *Motor Cycle News*, who published it as a funny little story in the paper. Unfortunately, Mrs Miggins was an avid reader of *MCN* and she didn't view it in quite the same, practical, way that I did. A few days later I received a bill through the post for a brand-new carpet.

I wasn't too keen on going back to the Isle of Man after that, but it was nothing to do with the wrath of Mrs Miggins. Quite simply, I thought that racing motorcycles there was a ridiculously dangerous thing to do for fun and nobody was offering me enough money to risk it in 1976. However, things changed the following year when the British Grand Prix was taken away from the Isle of Man on safety grounds and moved to Silverstone, leaving the TT as an independent international road race, which it remains to this day.

As it also remains to this day, the TT was still a hugely prestigious race for the manufacturers, and even though the majority of the top World Championship riders like Agostini, Sheene and Roberts had boycotted the event, Texaco Heron Suzuki were still going across and they expected me to be there with them. Pat Hennen had said yes and as a factory rider in my first season you can imagine the amount of pressure on me to join him – not to mention the lure of the start money on offer from the organisers. It is hard to imagine a modern-day MotoGP or even British Superbike team saying to a rider: 'You *have* to do the Isle of Man.' But back then they could squeeze you pretty hard and the bottom line was that your bike was going. If you didn't go and get on it, then somebody else probably would.

Barry was annoyed with me for saying yes but my opinion was that it's easy to take a stand against the TT if you're already earning plenty of money through other championships. Take modern-day guys like John McGuinness, Bruce Anstey, Ian Hutchinson and Michael Rutter: the risks those boys take at the TT are still huge but so are the potential rewards. They make a good living out of doing it so who has the right to tell them it's wrong? Of course, I hate the fact that the TT has taken so many friends away from me but I am also completely aware that they died doing what they wanted to do. Nobody is forcing anybody. You weigh it up in your own mind: the danger versus the reward – credibility, money and satisfaction. The equation is different for everybody and it can only be decided by that particular individual at that particular moment in time. I don't think it is for anybody else to judge them.

Personally, I watch the guys now and I think they are as brave and as talented as any of the men who have gone before them, so my respect for them is equal. To me it doesn't matter if you have won 26 TTs or just the one, or whether it was in 1967 or 2017. You were the fastest and the bravest on the day and you deserve all the accolades that are rightly thrown your way.

So back I went to the TT, along with a few other factory riders like Pat Hennen, Joey Dunlop, Mick Grant, John Williams and Phil Read, who were obviously the main men to beat, as well as some other really strong Irish riders like Tom Herron. Of course, now there isn't a single MotoGP rider who would even consider racing the TT and in BSB there are just a couple of competitive riders, like Peter Hickman and Josh Brookes, who choose to do it. But back in 1977 I'd say it was about a 50/50 split between the regular factory 500cc World Championship riders who went and those who stayed at home, and I looked up to them all.

I don't think there's any question that the best I ever came up against on the Isle of Man was Joey Dunlop. The man won 26 TTs in total, which remains the all-time record, so it is hard to argue with that. Joey's life revolved around the event, very much like his brilliant nephew Michael Dunlop now, and virtually any other race he competed in was designed to get him ready for those sacred two weeks on the island. Those

Dunlop boys have a love for road racing and a talent for road racing and the truth is you only really need to start out with one of those things; with a bit of luck and time, the other usually follows.

It was an honour for me to ride against Joey but personally my big TT hero was Mike Hailwood, a man many people still rate as the greatest ever motorcycle racer on the roads and short circuits. Unfortunately, I didn't get the chance to race against Mike because by the time I arrived he was already off car racing, and then when he made his comeback in 1979 it ironically gave me the opportunity to sit it out. There was no pressure on me from Suzuki that year precisely because they had signed Mike and they had actually offered him my spare Grand Prix bike to ride. I was asked by *MCN* what I thought about him coming back and I said I thought he was mad. Hailwood was a multiple World Champion and a legend of the sport, but I was convinced he couldn't come back and ride as hard as he had done in the past at a place like the Isle of Man. I wasn't the only one to say that, but he won the Senior race on my bike and made fools of us all. The debate about 'The Greatest of All Time' is a hotly contested one and ultimately it comes down to a matter of personal opinion. But to me, and to anybody I have spoken to who was fortunate enough to race against him, it is Mike Hailwood.

Mick Grant was another rider I looked up to and the best piece of advice I ever got at the TT came from him. There were two particularly bumpy sections back then: one was Cronk y Voddy and the other was the Sulby Straight. It is hard to describe how bad those bumps were on a TZ500 – you could literally barely keep the throttle open because the bike was jumping from one side of the track to the other. Mick knew a thing or two about the TT course, having broken the lap record multiple times on the way to his seven victories, so

I asked him to help me out and naturally I hung on his every word. I said: 'Mick, I can't keep the bike under control, it's all over the place on Sulby. Is there a line I should be on?'

'Yes,' he answered, in his blunt Yorkshire manner. 'Right down the centre of the road.'

'Why?' I asked. 'Is it smoother?'

'No,' he replied. 'But the hedges are further away.'

Those words probably saved my life in 1978. I was riding along with the steering damper turned to the maximum when all of a sudden my right hand stopped moving. I couldn't compute what was going on until I realised that the weld had broken on the handlebar and it was just loose in my hand. Fortunately I managed to shut the throttle and get the bike slowed down and just as it ground to a halt the handlebar completely fell off. When I got back I handed the throttle to Martyn Ogbourne, the crew chief at Suzuki GB, with the cables dangling off, and said: 'There you go mate, you might need that bit.'

In the seventies we raced in all weathers. It didn't matter if it was foggy, raining or gusty: the race started at 2 p.m. and that was it. I remember flying up the Mountain, flat out at 160mph and not being able to see fifty yards in front of me because of the fog, thinking: 'What am I doing here?' Racing in the rain on a short circuit is not too bad because you can work out the grip and check where the puddles are so that you can avoid them next time around, but on the Isle of Man there was no way of knowing all that because it is such a long way around. You could have three different kinds of rain around that place, come out of a corner and ride straight into a deluge. Now, thankfully, even if there's a brief shower they hold the race until the road is dry and that can only be a good thing.

My best year at the TT was in 1985, which as usual was a race of attrition and a few of the front guys broke down early in the race. I came around and saw P3 on my pit board, which inspired me to push harder than I normally ever would have done at the TT. With the crowd waving me on over the final lap I threw caution to the wind and rode my heart out to clinch third behind Joey Dunlop and Tony Rutter.

Back in those days, you came back in and parked your bike up against a fence post in a field, because there was no flat ground to mount a bike stand, and as I excitedly walked off to the podium I looked back to see my mechanic Dave Johnson banging the bike against the post. I should have really twigged that there was something up, but I was too busy enjoying the celebrations and looking forward to my first ever swig of the podium champagne at the TT. After the podium and the press conference I headed straight to the beer tent to begin the proper celebrations and I was just taking a sip of my first pint when I felt a tap on my shoulder.

The *Daily Telegraph* – Monday, 3 June 1985

Parrish excluded in 'oversize tank' row
by George Turnbull

STEVE PARRISH, 31, who finished third in the Formula 1 TT, yesterday threatened to leave the Isle of Man following a controversial ruling which could bar him from the results and cost him nearly £4,000.

After achieving his best placing in seven years of TT racing, it was alleged following a machine check that the fuel tank of Parrish's 750cc Mitsui Yamaha was 1.35 litres over the permitted maximum.

The clerk of the course immediately excluded him from the results and yesterday an international jury rejected Parrish's appeal.

The jury admitted, however, that Parrish had no advantage by having an oversized tank – he stops twice to refuel like other riders – and did not deliberately set out to circumvent the regulations.

But despite their obvious sympathy towards Parrish, the jury said it had no option but to confirm the decision of the clerk of the course.

Parrish, one of Britain's most popular riders, who had accumulated £3,900 in prize money over the six laps on Saturday, was furious at the jury's decision and initially decided to leave the island.

But last night he chose to stay to build up his case for an appeal to the International Motorcycle Federation within the next 15 days. However, he may not ride in two other races later this week.

Parrish maintains that the tank was of the correct size originally but after standing in the brilliant sunshine for more than four hours prior to the race the fuel in the 24-litre tank and the tank itself had expanded.

Experts confirm that can take place in hot conditions and Parrish said: 'If officials want to check tanks they should do so before the start of the race. As far as I am concerned, they now have to prove the tank did not expand in the heat.'

The controversy marred the Formula 1 race, won by World Champion Joey Dunlop.

We had taken that bike to Daytona in the March, where they also measured the tank and it was fine, but looking back I reckon Dave realised it was borderline and was trying to put a dent in it to reduce the capacity. Unfortunately, the tank on an FZ750 Yamaha was made out of steel so he didn't make even a tiny dink and I was flung out. I was gutted because I had risked my neck more than ever that day and had come away with nothing. I had never been on the podium at the

TT before and I knew I wasn't likely to be there again. Even a fourth place would have been my best result.

I have never been afraid to bend the rules but, genuinely, this wasn't the case on this occasion. I had stopped twice for fuel, just like everybody else, so there really wouldn't have been anything to gain by having a bigger tank, plus even the stewards recognised that I had three litres of fuel left anyway! To this day I truly believe that the tank expanded under the heat of the sun on the start line and I protested in all sorts of ways, getting engineers from Shell to write detailed reports on how this could have happened. Nobody protested – Tony Rutter even backed my claim to be reinstated – but it was all deemed irrelevant and my appeals were rejected. A rider called Sammy McClements was promoted to third place but even he said that he could not have beaten me that day and did not want me to be disqualified.

If there is one thing that annoys me more than being accused of cheating when I haven't, it is being out-cheated by somebody else when I have. In that respect, I have to take my hat off to Mick Grant, who out-cheated me at everything. Granty beat me to the 1985 British Superstock Championship by having me thrown out at Snetterton after accusing me of running illegal camshafts, which I didn't, although they did find a slight discrepancy on a tiny jet, which Mick later admitted made no difference whatsoever. Ten years ago I actually got to ride his bike from that season at Scarborough and found it had a factory ECU (engine control unit) on it. The scrutineers couldn't check the electronics back in those days but Mick was getting a good extra 300rpm out of that thing, so he properly out-did us there!

Other than that bittersweet race of 1985, if you look at my results from the TT they were all sevenths and eighths; I never really pushed that hard. I can look back now and admit that

I was running around there at a pace I was very comfortable at, but even that still scared me, I don't mind admitting it. The TT was the only race where I would travel over on the ferry, look up at the sky and think: 'I hope I come back home on this thing.' You wouldn't be travelling to Silverstone or Imola thinking anything like that. Accidents still happened at those places, of course, but it wasn't something that really ever crossed your mind. At the TT, you went out there and knew you had a fortnight of serious risk and only a certain amount of it was within your control. You had to hope and pray that you didn't hit a sheep or a pigeon or your tyre went flat.

I know that guys like Steve Hislop and Carl Fogarty, great short circuit racers, were extra proud of their TT wins because they'd had to stick their necks out that much further. The key to their success was managing the risk, which I suppose in a way is the same in any sport. If you swing for a six at cricket, for example, you are taking more of a risk than playing for a single but the rewards are much greater. The difference here is that the risk is not losing your wicket. It's losing your life.

In general, I always felt that my pre-race nerves at any circuit in the world were nothing to do with the fear of getting hurt. Everybody gets nervous about doing things that are important to them, but not because it is going to kill them if it goes wrong. As a racer it is because you don't want to fuck up in front of your team, your mechanics, your sponsors and – if you're really lucky – your fans. For me, the TT was an exception to that rule.

Mike Hailwood once said to me that the day you are not nervous is the day you should quit. But that wasn't a problem for me at the Isle of Man because I was shitting myself every time. To me it was a bit like exercise: before it starts you don't really want to do it, but once it's over you're like: 'Shit, that was good!' I know from my collection of silver replica trophies at home that I finished 13 races so considering the attrition rate at the TT, in terms of mechanical breakdowns, I must have entered at least twenty.

I don't know if I enjoyed a single one of them but I can clearly remember the adrenaline rush afterwards. Maybe the closest thing I can compare the feeling to is when you're driving along a country road in your car, you go too fast around a bend and everything *nearly* goes wrong. You know the one: you'd much rather it hadn't happened, but you can't deny the buzz you felt in the moments after it did! Well, that would happen ten times per lap on the TT course and you just knew that each one had been a brush with instant death. That's how it was, and no doubt still is.

Nowadays the bikes are more powerful and the speeds are much higher, but I feel I can still talk about today's races with at least a little understanding of what the guys are going through, so I absolutely love doing just that as part of the team that brings the coverage to ITV4 on every night of the TT. It is hard work but I get a great deal of satisfaction from it because there's something substantial to show at the end of each day. Sometimes in television you can spend all day filming a two-minute piece, but at the TT we have an hour-long daily programme that makes the whole thing so worthwhile. The riders are all friendly and approachable and the North One team are a fantastic bunch, from the producers to the presenters.

I first worked with Craig Doyle many years ago, when he first swapped the sandy beaches of *Holiday* on BBC1 for the greasy asphalt of the British Superbike pit-lane. Craig is great to work with – a lovely bloke and a true professional – and as a trained presenter, rather than a retired racer, he knows the value of asking the right questions of the experts, rather than trying to prove his own knowledge by giving the information himself. I think that helps us all do our jobs properly and if there's one thing for sure it's that Craig makes a better television presenter than he does a double-glazing salesman!

I also have the great pleasure of working regularly with James Whitham, who was an extremely talented and determined rider in his day and now makes for great company as a colleague both at the TT and when we spend nine long days together on stage at the NEC in November.

James Whitham – former British and World Superbike, Grand Prix and TT rider

My experience with Stavros has been mostly working with him, either on television or at the bike show every November at the NEC, and I suppose I am lucky not to have been on the end of too many of his pranks, apart from the usual daft stuff – like when he handed a waiter a note and asked him to deliver it to my wife Andrea. The note said: 'I am only a humble Albanian waiter but I have seen you, I fancy you and I know I can make you happy.' She looked at it, looked back at the kid and smiled and put the note in her handbag. She didn't even tell me about it until much later but still I was like: 'What the fuck?' Eventually Stavros owned up to it and we had a good laugh but, honestly, how he has not been beaten up before now I'll never know. The best one I saw happen was in Miami airport, on the way to the big Daytona 200 race in Florida. There was a little pop-up ice cream stall, manned by a lady who I can only describe as how you might imagine the woman in the Tom & Jerry cartoons to look, if you work your way up from her feet and ankles. She must have had twenty-five or thirty different flavours to choose from and she looked like she'd sampled them all. Anyway, while she was busy serving the customer in front of us Steve threw his retractable mouse into the mint choc-chip. Now, the key to these pranks is always in the timing, and sometimes he gets it perfect, sometimes he goes a bit early because he's so keen. This one was spot on: just as she reached forward with her scoop he hit the button and the fucking mouse shot across ten flavours of ice cream. This poor woman went absolutely mental and reeled backwards screaming: 'VERMIN! VERMIN!' She is the only twenty-stone woman I have ever seen scared of ice cream! Even when she hit the wall behind her, her legs were still going. If it had happened now, everybody would have got arrested, they'd have assumed it was some kind of terrorist attack, but we were well out of the way by the time the police came and taped off the area. He doesn't tend to panic much, Steve, because he has a good knack of getting out of a tight spot, but he was shitting himself a little bit then because he knew that if anybody had seen him he was bang in trouble.

The trick with the letter from the waiter is one of my all-time favourites but it did get me into massive trouble once on a night out with Barry and Steph, in Langan's Brasserie in London: the young lady's boyfriend took umbrage with the waiter, who pointed me out across the restaurant and the pair of them came charging straight at me. I didn't learn my lesson, of course, and poor James is just one of a number of irate boyfriends and confused waiters that I have managed to upset with that one over the years.

Along with Steve Plater, Cameron Donald and all the North One crew, we have a tight-knit team that I believe does a phenomenal job at the TT. We have a good laugh together but we all know what our role is during the day and you wouldn't believe the effort and graft that goes into each one of those shows. Personally, I think they should make a television programme about how they make the television programme! You have to get stuck in, big style, and there's a knife constantly against your throat to get the job done right because you are up against the clock. At 9 p.m. those credits are going to roll and there just has to be a programme ready to broadcast. Often they'll still be editing part two while part one is on air, and then part three when part two is on and so on. It's a crazy amount of stress for the producers to go through every day for two weeks but somehow it always seems to come off and it is incredibly satisfying when it does.

For me it's a little bit like riding the TT in that the graft and effort that goes into it pays dividends at the end. Our viewing figures of around 750,000 are better than anything else they have on ITV4, and the show has developed something of a cult following. At the end of May people know that the TT is coming up and characters like Guy Martin, with his best-selling books and his spin-off television shows, have opened the races out to a new audience, which I think is wonderful.

Guy gets a bit of stick from some of the other riders but I think generally it is in jest and although the TT win may have eluded him so far, the stardom certainly hasn't. I sometimes feel a bit sorry to see the likes of John McGuinness, a 23-time TT winner, getting pushed out of the way by fans wanting to get to Guy. It's a bit like when somebody other than Valentino Rossi wins at Mugello or Misano; the fans invade the track and won't go home until Rossi has appeared on the podium. I also feel sorry for many of those fans because even when they do get to meet Guy he rarely wants to speak to them, purely because he is trying to focus on his racing, and you have to respect that.

Overall there are many things that the Isle of Man has given me. As Barry put it in the opening line to his best man's speech at our wedding: 'Most people who come back with something from the Isle of Man have to go to a clinic to get rid of it. But Stavros has come back with a wife.' It would take far more than a clinic to get rid of Ruth, but I do still like to sit down sometimes and watch our wedding video in reverse, just so that at the end I can see her get in the car and fuck off.

Ruth and I first met in 1984 at a post-race TT party that I'd gatecrashed along with a couple of mates, where she was working as a hostess for BMW. I was still with my girlfriend Linda, I'm ashamed to admit, but Ruth and I ended up seeing quite a lot of each other – almost all of each other, in fact – back home in England and it all came to a head when I booked her into the Donington Manor Hotel in Castle Donington during a race meeting. Linda was staying at the circuit in the caravan but she got a tip-off from somebody and turned up at the bloody hotel! I managed to make a dash for it down the fire escape, but there was no denying what was going on and my long and happy relationship with Linda was finally over.

Many years later Linda and I became friends again, and I always appreciated the great support she gave me during the early part of my career, but at the time our break-up was acrimonious and awkward. Barry was pretty angry with me and Stephanie even more so, because over the years the four of us had spent so much time together. We were like a little family, I suppose, but Ruth and I were getting on great, I liked her friends and as soon as I saw the big family estate up in Lincolnshire, I proposed straight away! A year later, on 18 August 1985, we were married at the St Mary and St Gabriel parish church in Binbrook, Lincolnshire.

Our wedding was a big event, with over two hundred guests, and I remember coming out of the church to see the streets lined with people and photographers. It seemed the whole village had come out for a nosey, although, of course, they weren't out to see Ruth or me. Lincolnshire has always had a particularly strong motorcycling community so as far as the locals were concerned it was a star-studded guest list, with the likes of Roger Burnett and Wayne Gardner (in a daft white suit) there, not to mention my best man.

Barry Sheene was one of the most famous men in the country but that didn't impress Ruth's well-to-do Lincolnshire farming family. The pair of us had both crashed in the Swedish Grand Prix at Anderstorp the weekend before and we looked like a right pair of daft invalids walking into the church; me with a severe limp and Barry with the aid of a walking stick. You can just imagine that the opening line of his speech went down like a fart in a lift and it didn't do anything to dispel the bad impression those posh folks had of us dirty bikers.

I managed to further remove myself from their affections just before Christmas that year with what was probably my biggest and easily my most stupid prank yet. Naturally, it is the one I am most proud of.

15

Out with a bang

It is fair to say that I first questioned the wisdom of marriage as soon as the morning after our wedding day, when Ruth's friend, Barbara Scott, a very attractive British Airways stewardess, brought us a cup of tea in bed wearing nothing but an apron. For Ruth, the moment of enlightenment probably came later that week on our 'honeymoon', which we spent in the van, with my mechanic 'Mushroom' Johnson driving us down to Misano for the San Marino Grand Prix. But if those romantic few days on the Adriatic coast in the back of a Transit hadn't quite piqued Ruth's regret, then she would be finally forced to admit that her family were right about me all along just three months later, when I eventually returned from an eventful last race of the season in Macau.

Whether you raced on two wheels or four, the Macau Grand Prix was and still is every racer's ultimate busman's holiday. Held annually in November since 1954, it was the only event to jointly host motorcycle and Formula 3 races but since it didn't count as a round of either World Championship it was a fantastic opportunity at the end of the season for both paddocks to go out and enjoy themselves. Young drivers like Ayrton Senna, Michael Schumacher and David Coulthard would be there racing in F3 and for those guys it was a hugely prestigious event where many of them first made their names. For us bike racers it was just a great excuse for an end-of-season blow-out.

The driving force behind the whole thing was a tiny bloke with big ideas called Teddy Yip, a billionaire businessman known as the 'Grand Old Man of Macau'. Teddy was born in Indonesia, which at the time would have been the Dutch East Indies, a colony of the Netherlands. As a Dutch national he was educated in Europe and learned several languages before returning to Asia in the 1940s, building up an empire of travel agencies, hotels, casinos and trading companies in Hong Kong. Developing Macau was his passion project and along with a few business partners they transformed the place into a major tourist destination, running a monopoly on the hotels and casinos and the ferry and hydrofoil service from Hong Kong.

With such a huge appetite for gambling over the border in China, Macau became a gold mine and even now it is ahead of Las Vegas as the world leader in gambling revenue. So it's fair to say that Teddy wasn't short of a few quid, some of which he spent on car racing, competing himself for many years before employing the likes of Ayrton Senna, Nelson Piquet, Mika Hakkinen, Alan Jones and Keke Rosberg. They drove for him during the early part of their careers in the Macau Grand Prix and then he entered a car in a number of Formula 1 races. The event started as a treasure hunt around the streets of the peninsula in the 1950s but over the years Teddy and his boys had developed it into one of the most famous motorsport events in the world and it was a central part of the tourist industry there.

As you might expect, Teddy was a colourful character, with a penchant for fast women that rivalled his love of fast cars, and he loved to throw a party. I heard some great stories about him, like the time he celebrated gaining entries to a Formula 1 race at Long Beach and the Indianapolis 500 by throwing a bash for 800 people on the *Queen Mary*, but bringing in his own chefs from Macau because the catering wasn't up to his standard. He had his cars lifted onto the deck of the ship to show them off to his guests and missed the technical inspection as a result, picking up a $10,000 penalty that he just laughed off and paid.

To be honest, the motorcycle racing was kind of second division in Macau and I worked out pretty early on that all the best parties were being thrown for the car folks. Having said that, these parties were so big you probably didn't really need an invitation (there might be two thousand people sitting down in the casino hotel for dinner), but since I was friends with the likes of Damon Hill, Eddie Jordan and an Irish driver called Tommy Byrne, who was something of a party animal himself, I'd usually tag along with them.

Every year Teddy would invite a superstar celebrity to be the guest of honour, who was usually a Hollywood actor like James Garner, really famous at the time for being in *The Rockford Files*, a series about a private investigator who lived in a dilapidated static caravan in a car park in Malibu. I remember sitting with Tommy and Eddie and a few others, tucking into the prawns and caviar and slugging back the champagne, when Tommy, in his wonderful Irish accent, leaned over to James Garner and said: 'This has got to be better than that fucking caravan you live in!'

Another flash event we got invited to was a cocktail party on the lawns of Teddy's mansion. Everybody who was anybody in Macau at the time was there sipping champagne, with these beautiful models wandering around serving packets of Marlboro cigarettes, who sponsored Teddy's F1 team, on silver trays. On this occasion Gene Hackman was the star guest and my mate Bernard Murray, a fellow bike racer who was a big Hackman fan, spent about an hour plucking up the courage to sidle over to him and try to strike up a conversation. Eventually he got his chance to step in, at which point he said: 'Gene, I just wanted to say I thought you were fantastic in *Midnight Cowboy*.'

There was a lovely, pregnant pause before Hackman turned to Bernard and replied: 'I wasn't in it.'

Poor Bernard didn't bother to say anything else; he just turned around and walked back over to us. Of course, we were in absolute stitches and he has not lived it down to this day.

Our annual trips out to Macau were organised by Mike Trimby, a former racer who competed there and actually finished on the podium with me on our first visit in 1978. Mike had an entrepreneurial streak and came up with the smart idea of setting himself up as an agent to the Macau tourist board and from 1982, when they decided to make the bike race a much bigger deal, he was bringing around twenty-five riders over, including some of the biggest names in our sport like Kevin Schwantz, Wayne Gardner, Carl Fogarty, Ron Haslam and the late Joey and Robert Dunlop, all of them enticed by the bonus of a holiday in Thailand on the way home. The company was called Planet Travel, although we called it Trimby Tours, and basically Mike was given a budget and would pay the riders a fee and organise the tickets, freight, accommodation and everything else. On top of that he would sell the trip to punters too, so it was a very clever and, I imagine, lucrative little operation that understandably he didn't want anybody screwing up.

There were definitely no rules off the track but Trimby always reminded us of what was expected on it, and the number one priority was to look after yourself. A serious accident would have been bad for business and the circuit was so bloody dangerous on a bike. There was absolutely no run-off, just Armco barriers and concrete walls to stop the cars from crashing into the sea, which frankly would have been preferable for us. Not many motorcycle racers crashed at Macau and got away with it, so certain guys whom Trimby judged to be 'win or bin' merchants back home in the UK never even got the invitation to compete. As the founding member of the self-preservation society, however, I was asked back every year. And with my main focus on the beachwear rather than the silverware, I always made extra sure I stayed in one piece.

Probably the only rider I ever saw take it really seriously was a Japanese lad called Sadao Asami. He'd been sent by Yamaha to win the race for the factory and it seemed to me that he would have been happier to crash and kill himself than return home as a dishonourable loser. I finished second behind Asami on three consecutive occasions in 1978, 1979 and 1980, which was no disgrace, and I can guarantee that I was enjoying the experience a whole lot more than he will have done.

Over the years I learned not to get too carried away with the parties, mainly after an incident in the 1982 race when I had such a bad hangover from the night before that I just fell off the bike. I'd met some people who lived out there and they had got me terribly drunk on this Portuguese brandy. Normally when you come off a motorcycle you know why or how it happened, especially when you're riding well within the limit like we did at Macau. But I'd ended up upside down and the only reason I could think of was that I had been drunk the night before. Like I said, not many people got away with a crash at Macau but, as usual, I came up smelling of roses as well as brandy. It was the first time I ever tried riding with a hangover and I made sure never to try it again.

In retrospect, our trip out there in 1985 was probably doomed from the journey over onwards, which started off in typical style, with Bernard Murray and his mechanic Malcolm 'Chad' Chadwick travelling down from Manchester to meet up with me and Dave Johnson at Church Farm. From there we headed down to Charlwood via Southampton Row in London, where we stopped by the Allan and Allan joke shop and pretty much bought the place out; everything from exploding cigarette lighters and plastic dog turds to stink bombs. There's no way they'd allow you to travel with all those combustibles in your suitcase nowadays but ours were packed with the stuff. As usual we parked up at Barry and Steph's, had a couple of gin and tonics with them and then headed on to Gatwick. Barry never made it to Macau – I don't think Trimby ever put him on the entry list: firstly because the circuit was so dangerous, secondly because his asking fee would have pushed even Teddy Yip's budget to the limit and thirdly because the level of off-track misdemeanours would have trebled overnight.

Even though Barry wasn't coming he delivered us to the airport and even got us into the business class lounge, where we all proceeded to get way too drunk. Almost as soon as the plane started levelling out we delved into our bag of tricks and somebody let off a 'dirty drains' stink bomb. The stench was horrendous; everybody was gagging and putting their napkins over their faces, while the stewardesses were running around in a genuine state of panic. Supposedly there had been a recent air disaster caused by some idiot lighting a camping stove on board to cook his lunch, if you can believe that.

So we'd only just taken off when an announcement came over the tannoy that due to a suspected gas leak we were diverting to make an emergency landing at Frankfurt. In the end somebody had to put their hand up and even though I automatically got the blame from Trimby I spent twenty years protesting my innocence until we finally found out it was Chad.

All the usual suspects were on that flight to Hong Kong: me, Dave, Bernard and Chad, Mick Grant, Trevor Nation and Ron Haslam, a brilliant Belgian called Didier de Radiguès and the craziest German I ever met, Gustav Reiner, an enthusiastic rider who was never scared to crash apart from at Macau. Gustav would actually almost miss the race that year after commandeering a state tour bus, sticking the driver's hat on and taking an excursion across the border to China. Once they'd managed to prise him out of the driving seat he threw fireworks out of the windows into the paddy fields, causing the water buffaloes to stampede.

My usual routine was to spend the first night in Hong Kong where the local Yamaha importer Mr Mok, a personal sponsor of mine for the Macau races, would organise a big dinner. As the top Yamaha rider I was the guest of honour and thus I was presented with a specially cooked chicken's head by Mr Mok, which I was expected to eat in front of the assembled company but which routinely made its way into somebody's jacket pocket or handbag.

From Hong Kong we made the trip across the South China Sea to Macau, usually by ferry on the way out because it was a lot cheaper, although invariably we jumped on the hydrofoil back because there was usually a reason to leave in a hurry. Our accommodation was a plush hotel near the Macau horse racing course, on the other side of a long causeway from the main part of the peninsula where the Guia racetrack was located. We would need transport to get us there and back and we always knew just where to get it.

The man we knew simply as 'Mr Moke' was no relation to Mr Mok the Yamaha dealer. In fact he was a retired English policeman from Manchester who had poured his and his wife's life savings into starting their own business – hiring out Mini Mokes (an open-top jeep built mainly from parts off an Austin Mini) to tourists in Hong Kong and Macau. However, Mr Moke had discovered to his cost that motorcycle racers are a very particular kind of tourist, certainly not the kind to take good care of your hire car fleet, so he was reluctant to let any of us use his vehicles.

I know this because he told me so himself, when we met entirely by coincidence over a beer in a local 'establishment'. We recognised each other because I had just hired one of his Mokes, although he hadn't realised at the time that I was a racer, and he spent most of our conversation telling me all about these hooligans that came to Macau every year and damaged his cars and, subsequently, his business. I agreed that these were a most unsavoury kind of people who were not to be trusted, a point that was underlined when I went to leave and found my Mini Moke turned upside down on the pavement outside with oil, water and battery acid pissing out of it and running down the street! We both had a pretty good idea who was to blame, and Mr Moke was not impressed.

The race itself that year was relatively uneventful, with Ron Haslam carefully tip-toeing to the win while I took fifth place on my FZ750 Yamaha. More importantly, with the Grand Prix now out of the way, it was time to get down to the serious business of the weekend.

Close to the circuit there was a place where they made all of the fireworks for Chinese New Year and I was like a kid in a sweetshop. They had this enormous contraption that looked like a small barrel, about a couple of feet in diameter and a couple of feet high, and only cost about a pound, so I invested in about ten of the things. Along with a couple of accomplices, we came up with a plan to roll one of them into the local massage parlour on the Sunday night, when we knew a bunch of riders and mechanics would be in there 'relaxing' after the race.

It was decided that I would be the getaway driver and Howard Lees, a journalist who was also a decent rider, would be on lookout. Paul Butler, who went on to hold the very distinguished role of MotoGP Race Director but at the time was in charge of the factory Yamaha team, was tasked with lighting the blue touch paper, which he duly did with the end of his trademark cigar, before we rolled it straight through the sliding glass doors into the entrance of the establishment.

The man in the firework shop had done us proud: a bit like the girls in the parlour he had promised us a big bang and we definitely got one! This thing went off like you can't believe – rockets and red tape were flying out in all directions as it whizzed, banged, exploded and smoked the whole place out. The scene resembled something from a *Carry On* film, with semi-naked girls running out of the building, followed quickly by a bunch of semi-naked blokes – most of whom we knew.

According to the plan, this was the moment we were to make our escape but it was such a hilarious sight we couldn't help but stand back and admire our handiwork. Sadly, our complacency proved to be our downfall, because sitting at the bar, sipping on a cold beer, was the chief of police's personal driver. I don't know about getting a back-hander – the chief was more likely in one of the rooms getting a front-hander – but crucially his driver had seen the whole thing unfold and got a good look at us.

When we did finally sneak off and jump into our getaway vehicle, which was the minibus Trimby had hired for the whole group that weekend, we were accompanied by an Ulsterman called Billy who had been sat next to the driver at the bar and unwisely decided he wanted to join our gang! After an hour or so of drinking, laughing and regaling anybody who'd listen with our exploits in the hotel bar, the doors flew open and in burst what seemed like the entire Macau police force.

Mike Trimby – former motorcycle racer and owner of Planet Travel

There was something different every year. I remember once staying in the Hyatt hotel in Hong Kong and I was getting harangued by the concierge, who was claiming that one of my party had been moving furniture around, which I steadfastly denied. Just at that exact moment the lift doors opened and there was Stavros, with the whole lift stacked to the top with upturned chairs and tables. He looked at me and shrugged and then the lift doors closed and he disappeared. Anyway, on that particular night in Macau I had just got into bed at the hotel with my wife Irene and was saying to her how good that year's group had been, when we got a phone call from reception saying: 'The police are here – your people have blown up a hotel!' I couldn't believe it, but I went down and was told how three of my party had rolled this huge explosive into the massage parlour and deafened twenty of the girls, before making their escape in a van from a rental company in Hong Kong that was under my name. They had a positive ID on Paul Butler because he had a distinctive white beard at the time and he'd been the one seen lighting the fuse, and they quickly rounded up the rest of them. They were just whisking everybody off when over comes this Irish bloke, Billy, who I only knew to be a mechanic of Neil 'Smutty' Robinson. As far as I knew he wasn't even involved but he insisted, 'If they're going, I'm going with them!' and off they went. The four of them got released that night and the following morning we were in the lobby getting ready to leave for Thailand, with everybody chuckling and laughing because they thought the whole thing was all over, when suddenly the police turned up again. This time Stavros did a runner, leaving Butler, Lees and Billy behind. There was a huge drama and the police were telling me they wanted Parrish back or else nobody was getting out, but by the time I got to speak to Stavros he didn't care. He told me he'd be in Europe before those guys saw Hong Kong again, so I had to lay it on thick.

Obviously I didn't share our new comrade Billy's sense of fellowship when the police came bursting back into the hotel that morning so I quickly grabbed Dave Johnson's baseball hat and dashed up the stairs to the first floor. I jumped down the fire escape ladder, ran around to the back of the hotel, grabbed a cab and headed for the port. I always kept an old passport with me for just this kind of eventuality and that was the one I'd handed to the police the night before, even though it had the corner snipped off, so I had no problems jumping on the first hydrofoil back to Hong Kong.

I'd been sitting on the pier at the other end, sipping gin and tonics, for a few hours when the next hydrofoil eventually appeared on the horizon. I pictured Paul, Howard and Billy on board, having spent a while explaining themselves to the police and probably having to pay for a new floor in the parlour, while Trimby would no doubt be annoyed with me, but that was nothing new. It wouldn't be long before we were all sunning ourselves on a beach in Pattaya and, as always, all would be forgiven. How wrong I was!

Trimby told me in no uncertain terms that I needed to get my stupid arse back to Macau. Paul, Howard and Billy were all locked up and they were threatening to impound the freight from the Grand Prix – motorcycles, cars and all. According to Trimby, he'd cut a deal with the police so that the rest of them could leave, but the prisoners and the freight were all staying put until I went back and handed myself over. If that wasn't enough, Butler was due in Hong Kong that day to sign the biggest ever sponsorship deal in the history of Grand Prix motorcycle racing with tobacco giants Lucky Strike and if I didn't go back and sort this thing out there were millions of pounds about to go up in smoke.

I weighed up the options and figured I didn't have any. No sooner had I docked back in Macau than I saw my passport picture, blown up and pinned on a notice board by the hydrofoil departure gate, and I knew I was in trouble. Sure enough, the police were on standby and I was handcuffed and taken straight to jail. It's hard to really describe how horrible the conditions were there, but let's just say it's not a place I would recommend for a holiday and after three or four days the joke had well and truly worn off for all parties.

The police had left us to stew for a while but really they just seemed interested in getting a good deal to secure our release. Eventually we agreed to fork out for the fire damage and the cleaning up of the premises. We got a further bill from the parlour for loss of earnings, which was a bloody cheek considering how much money we'd put behind the counter during the week before, and then another one from Hertz for the van, which had been held back in Macau as evidence and then couldn't be shipped back to Hong Kong because the temporary export licence had expired. In the end we had to agree to buy the thing and as far as I know we still own it, although I am sure it has long since gone to rot on a scrap heap in Macau! Anyway, once all the money was handed over we were free to go, although those four days in a Chinese prison were nothing compared to what awaited me when I flew home to face Ruth! We had only been married a few months and she wasn't the most understanding at the best of times, so after this incident I reckon she was questioning her own sanity as much as mine.

Macau Sports Post – **Wednesday, 19 November 1986**

Parrish bang on course for a grand exit in Macau
by Barry Grindrod

FORMER British motorcycle champion Steve Parrish is look-ing to finish his professional racing career with a bang on Saturday in the Macau Grand Prix.

But, he insisted yesterday, the fireworks this year will be confined strictly to the track.

Following last year's race Parrish and a couple of other riders were detained for three days in Macau and had their passports seized after letting off firecrackers in a local mas-sage parlour.

It was an incident that prompted a headline in Britain's *Motor Cycle News* of 'Gang Bang Goes Wong'.

'Someone suggested that this year we use dynamite but I decided I'm going to handcuff myself to the tour operator,' laughed Parrish.

But joking aside, Parrish said he would dearly love to end his distinguished 10-year professional career on a winning note aboard his 750cc Loctite Yamaha.

'I always said I wanted to retire while I was still riding well,' he said. 'I didn't want to just peter out slipping further and further down the field.'

The knocks are also beginning to hurt more, he added. Over the years, Parrish has broken a leg, an ankle, a wrist and a collarbone twice. 'The bones take longer to heal as you get older and the old injuries tend to niggle,' said the 33-year-old Parrish.

'Only this morning I was playing squash and the leg I broke last year was playing up. But I've no regrets, I would not have done anything else. People don't believe me when I say this will be my last race. I'm not saying categorically that I will not race a bike again but this is the end of my professional career. I may make the occasional guest appearance.'

Parrish described Macau as a great winding down event to the Grand Prix season – but if he takes the chequered flag on Saturday what's the betting that there will be more than champagne corks popping.

It's hard to imagine *MCN* using such creative language nowadays but despite the dodgy headlines, and even though I was officially banned from Macau until it was handed back to Chinese sovereignty in 1999, Trimby somehow got me back in for my last ever professional motorcycle race at the end of the 1986 season, funnily enough on a Yamaha with the appropriately named Lucky Strike sponsorship that Paul Butler had managed to secure on his release from jail. The whole deal came about at the very last minute and I had just a couple of weeks to find some teammates and paint up the bikes in Lucky Strike colours. Kenny Irons and Keith Huewen were both up for it so we got Kenny's Loctite Yamaha and Keith's own Suzuki GSX-R750 all sprayed up and off we went for one last hurrah. Again it would be Ron Haslam who took the win, and while Kenny challenged for a podium and Keith and I tottered around counting down the laps, once again the weekend would prove to be far more memorable for events off the track than on it.

Mick Grant – Macau Motorcycle Grand Prix winner 1977 and 1984

I wasn't involved in the execution of the 'gunpowder plot' in 1985 but I was there when they were planning it and I was in the hotel when the police came around looking for Stavros. It was a serious deal at the time but the whole thing didn't seem to put him off and I remember the following season being back in Macau and going out for a meal with him and some Portuguese friends that I had over there. They took us down to the shanty town for some great local street food, where there were buckets outside the front of the restaurants with fresh fish and prawns flopping about in them. We came across one with these huge black toads in, so of course Stavros grabbed a couple of them and a big slippery eel – not to eat, of course, but to have a bit of fun with. I can remember I was driving this twelve-seater van full of people back to the hotel when one of the bloody toads escaped. I daren't put the brakes on in case I squashed the poor thing! Thankfully we got it back in one piece and Stavros managed to get the key to a journalist called Chris Carter's room and released the frogs in his bath and the eel in his toilet. We were downstairs having a drink in the bar when he called down. 'Get those fucking things out of my bathroom!' he was screaming. It makes me laugh now thinking of the sight of him looking down on the toads as he stepped into the bath. I honestly don't know which one of them would have been more frightened! He's a bugger is Stavros!

I'm always amazed, even nowadays, how easy it is to walk up to reception in a hotel and ask for a room key. It is very rare that they will ask you to produce any identification; mostly they'll just ask for your name and room number and hand over a key. In Macau, given that they barely spoke any English, it was enough to tell them the room number and that was it.

You can just imagine that when I came home and told Brownie about everything we were getting up to over in Macau it was only a matter of time before he made an appearance, and in 1986 he came over with his friend Chris. They arrived completely exhausted after a 24-hour flight and crashed out in their rooms, so as well as getting Chris Carter with the frogs I managed to get hold of their key and released a bucket load in their room too. When they eventually woke up they were surrounded by these things croaking and jumping around everywhere! Brownie even came back from the track that evening to find another one hiding in his wash bag.

Unfortunately, I wasn't the only person to take advantage of the hotel's open door policy and it was on that final trip in 1986 that Trimby got his own back on me. I was in my room at the hotel in Hong Kong when there was a knock at the door. I opened it up to be confronted by a senior-looking police officer, who said: 'We have reason to believe that you are carrying drugs and I would like to conduct a search on your room.' I had nothing to hide so I waved him in and said: 'Go for it!' Sure enough, a few moments later he pulled this big bag of white powder out of my toolbag. 'What's this then?' he said, before keying the bag open and sampling a little taste. 'Cocaine!' he exclaimed, before handcuffing me to the bed and disappearing to call the drug squad in.

Of course, I knew the bag must have been planted there by somebody but I couldn't be sure if it was a practical joke or a genuine plant. And obviously I had no way of knowing that it was actually just flour. Either way, I wasn't hanging around to find out so as soon as he had gone I dragged the bed over to the phone and managed to punch in the numbers down to the bar, where I knew Dave Johnson was having a drink. 'Dave, get yourself up here quick,' I said. As it happened, because I had refused to pay to transport all of the tools in the hold we had a fair amount of kit in this bag, so Dave whipped out a hacksaw and started grinding away at the handcuffs.

Moments later Trimby and all the guys involved in the set-up, including the policeman, who was also a rider in the Macau Grand Prix, burst into the room and pissed themselves laughing. It was a good get and I couldn't have been more relieved to see them. Much like *Beadle's About*, I had a fair idea something was afoot but I couldn't be 100 per cent sure – and the last thing I needed was another spell in a Chinese prison!

16

To 'The Squadron'

Michelle Hunter – Steve's fiancée

As the person closest to Steve I am always in the firing line and whenever he goes away for work or whatever, I know there is something, somewhere, waiting to explode or jump out on me. A couple of years ago I was going for an interview for a marketing job with a local company and I had got some samples together and made a presentation in a nice folder. I left it on the kitchen side overnight and the next morning I took it along to the interview. Everything was going well, I was chatting away with this guy and I said: 'I've brought a presentation folder for you to look at.' It never occurred to me to look inside it before I passed it over. The guy opened it up and went bright red. I thought, 'What the hell's wrong with him?' and when I looked down on the table Steve had put a load of leaflets for penile dysfunction and other sexual problems in the folder. Luckily I kind of knew the guy and he knew who my partner was so even though he was clearly embarrassed we kind of laughed it off. But I was mortified and I got really hot and started to itch, so I excused myself and went to the bathroom. Once I got there I realised Steve had put Velcro on the inside of all my underwear, and that was why I had got so uncomfortable when I got hot. Amazingly, I still got the job, but I didn't find it very funny. I should be used to it but sometimes I forget and I'll come in and there's cling film over the toilet bowl or a cup of cold water balanced on the shower door. I suppose it's what I've signed up for! Life would be quite boring otherwise. I do occasionally manage to get one up on Steve, like the surprise sixtieth birthday party I organised for him. Steve isn't the most inquisitive of people so hiding it from him wasn't so hard. I'd prearranged for his close friend John Brown and his wife Sue to collect us, saying they were taking us out for Steve's birthday. On picking us up, John told Steve that he had to stop at Minstrel Court to start his daughter Georgie's car as she had a flat battery. Prior to this I'd engaged Terry's wife Donna Rymer to help decorate and be in charge of the set-up of the party, which she did a grand job of, even picking up the two cakes I'd had specially made: one shaped like an RG500 in Texaco Heron Suzuki colours and the other a toilet complete with fake dog poo, fart machine, Billy Bob teeth and toilet roll. On arrival at Minstrel Court, John instructed Steve to go in and find Georgie while he started on the car. So Steve inno-cently walked straight in, jump leads in hand, to be met by a load of flashing cameras and a big cheer. For once, he was totally speechless. In front of him were his family, friends, teammates and mechanics from the biking and truck racing worlds – I even got hold of Mari Wilmott, his nanny from Church Farm when he was a boy, and his ex-girlfriend Linda and ex-wife Ruth just for good measure! Steve wouldn't let anyone cut the RG500 cake so it had pride of place on the kitchen worktop for months until it was eventually given a traditional send-off with stage maroons and a ceremonious explosion in the garden.

I live this lunatic life by choice, because I love giggling and laughing. And I love to have other people around me giggling and laughing too. It's my fuel, it's what keeps me going, and Michelle is usually full of it. We first properly met at her pub, the Queen Adelaide in Croydon, although we kind of knew each other before that because her kids went to the same school as mine. We had both just recently been divorced and I was having a quiet pint in the pub and we hit it off. Our wedding was originally set for 14 August 2053, to coincide with the golden anniversary of our first date and my hundredth birthday, but the likelihood is that by the time you read this book we will already be wed. After she has proofread some of the stories, I figure it will be the least I can do! In all seriousness, Michelle is the love of my life and she helps keep me smiling pretty much all of the time – often at her own expense, bless her.

I'm not saying I can't be a miserable bastard at times but usually I can turn almost any negative into a positive. I even laugh when I'm in pain – how weird is that? I can hurt myself, I can be rolling around in agony with a broken ankle and then burst out laughing. I lie to myself. I think: 'Well, that's the best outcome because of this . . . ' The way I looked at my retirement from racing was: 'Thank God I don't ever have to sit on a grid shitting myself again.' I turned my focus to being a team manager and then when the truck racing thing happened I thought, 'Brilliant!' and I focused on that. And when that started to dry up I saw it as an opportunity to work more with the BBC. When the BBC lost the MotoGP contract at the end of the 2013 season I just thought: 'Fine, I'm glad I'm not getting on an aeroplane to Qatar this weekend because it means I can be racing a car at Silverstone instead.'

I always try to find ways of making things right in my head and it has helped me stay away from issues like depression, which affects so many men of a certain age, over the years.

I never felt that mentally I got into a state that I couldn't turn around. I can see why people like Carl Fogarty have had issues when they've stopped racing. I can only imagine being as popular as he was, as successful as he was, and then being forced to retire and suddenly it all stops overnight. Suddenly you don't have that adrenaline from winning, you don't have the plaudits you crave, and then what have you got? What can possibly ever get you back to those heights?

I was never going to be a World Champion because I didn't have the killer instinct like Foggy, or Barry Sheene or Valentino Rossi. Racing together for so many years, I always felt I had as much talent as Barry but I didn't have his determination. Even when I was dominating truck racing, I never once went to a racetrack thinking: 'Right, I'm going to win today.' I was completely the opposite. I went along thinking: 'Well, if I can get in the top four that would be good; if I can win it's a bonus.' I was a percentage man. I never liked the idea of having victory set in my mind and then having to deal with the consequences of defeat. I never could face that. I would rather be surprised to win than be surprised to lose.

I am still like that in everything I do; I hate it when things don't turn out as well as they might. I never try to make a fast buck, I am not a gambler, and I think to win a World Championship you have to be prepared to take gambles. Ultimately, to win it all you have to be prepared to lose it all. And I suppose I have been prepared to sacrifice the ultimate highs in life in order to avoid the ultimate lows. I mean that in both a physical and a mental sense and in that respect I don't think I'm that strange at all. In fact, I think I am quite normal, and I have met other sportspeople just like me.

I was lucky that certain opportunities came up, but I was also careful never to look back and to always manufacture a positive scenario for the future. I get bored very easily and

in the winter months if I feel I'm not utilising my time properly I come up with something constructive to do. Like in the
November of 1994 I got up one morning feeling bored, so I
drove down to my local flying club and signed up for some
lessons. I suppose having just about exhausted every form of
transport on the ground, it was only a matter of time before I
took to the skies and just two months later I had my licence. I
was fortunate that I didn't have a job to go to during the week
so I was able to invest a lot of time into getting my minimum
forty hours of flight time and I sailed through the written
exams because they stupidly sat me in a room at Fowlmere
with all the text books on the shelf. As soon as I got my licence
I bought a plane, which I called Plummet Airways, and it has
been running out of the airstrip at the back of my little house
on Dave Morris's farm ever since.

Some of my early flights were pretty scary, more so when I
look back now because I realise that I didn't really know what
I was doing. The hardest thing in those early days compared
to now was that there was no GPS; you had a map and a whiz
wheel to plot your route according to the wind speed and direction, and then you drew a line on the map with a chinagraph
pencil and tried your best to follow it. I'd fly in all sorts of
weather with the wrong instruments, but to me at the time
it still just seemed so much safer than racing motorbikes so
I didn't think too much of it. I remember on one occasion I
offered to fly a bunch of television colleagues to Assen, in the
Netherlands, but shortly beforehand I broke my right hand in
a road bike accident so I decided to fly one-handed. Stupidly
I'd thought it would be easy but obviously it's not because as
well as operating the controls you also have to tune the radio
and everything else. I didn't realise this until I'd taken off so
understandably my passengers were rather nervous as they
ended up having to assist with flying the plane.

During the ash cloud in 2010 all of the commercial flights were grounded but the double World Superbike champion Troy Corser, a tough and wiry straight-talking Australian who is married to my old girlfriend Linda's daughter Sam, had to get over to Assen for a Superbike World Championship round there. Troy and Sam live not far away from me so they called me up and asked if Plummet Airways could help. 'No problem,' I said, and simply put a pair of Michelle's tights over the air intake. We had a lovely peaceful flight over to Groningen – every air traffic control we tried to contact was shut down because there weren't any other aircraft in the sky! But there was really nothing to worry about and we made it no problem, with a nice gentle landing at Groningen and a similarly peaceful return trip.

Not all of our flights have gone quite so well, though, and one year Michelle and I were going to the Isle of Man for the TT and it was blowing a gale. But the skies were clear so I decided to go for it and we left Liverpool for a flight that would normally take around half an hour. We tuned our radio in to the automated weather broadcast from Ronaldsway and we could hear that there were a couple of FlyBe flights going in ahead of us.

'Forty-two knots gusting forty-eight from the south-west,' came the report. The FlyBe captains weren't sure.

'Well, we'll keep coming at the moment but that's beyond our limitations,' was the gist of their replies.

The first flight had about six minutes to run before they finally decided to abort, turning back to Newcastle, and then the second one that was coming in from Belfast turned back too.

I checked in. 'This is Golf Mike India Charlie India . . .'

'Have you been listening to the weather updates?'

'Yes, I've been listening,' I said.

'And you're still coming, are you?'

'Yes, I'm still coming.'

'Okay, well everybody else has turned around and gone home so you're our number one priority. You can come in on runway two-six.'

It was a really funny wind and I couldn't get into it. We were being thrown around a fair bit so while Michelle got the iPad out to use as a black box I was still feeling quite convinced I could fly in there and turn in at the last minute. We had got to about ten miles out so I had started landing procedures, turned the autopilot off and started to line everything up when the message came through. 'Golf Mike India Charlie India: right-hand orbit.' For those of you unfamiliar with the jargon, that means 'turn around'.

I said: 'I thought you said I was number one?'

'You are still number one,' came the reply, 'but we're just preparing the fire engines.'

Needless to say, my confidence waned a little at this news but I managed to muddle the thing down to the ground and keep it there, despite the best efforts of the wind to blow us over. Even the firemen looked disappointed, with all their gear on and nothing to do.

On another occasion, flying to the Isle of Man, I was just passing over Liverpool when the autopilot switched itself off. I thought 'that's funny' so I went to reset it, and just as I was doing that the radio switched off too. I looked at the battery reading and we had about 8 volts, when it should have been 13, so clearly the alternator had packed in and we weren't getting any power into the battery. I was in the middle of Liverpool's airspace and probably should have just landed there but I needed to get over the water for the TT, so we carried on and switched everything off in the hope that we'd have just enough power to get the wheels down. It was a tense half hour over the Irish Sea until we got about three miles from Ronaldsway, when I flicked the power back on, got the wheels down and then just had enough power left to radio in and get clearance to land. A day or two later I was doing some television stuff on the start line at the TT and a bunch of lads who turned out to be firemen from Ronaldsway came over saying: 'We love you, you're the only person we ever have to get out for!'

Despite my reputation, there is never any shortage of volunteers wishing to save themselves a full day of travel to somewhere like Le Mans, where you would normally have to endure the delights of Paris Charles de Gaulle Airport or several hours on Eurostar and other trains. The bonus of just a couple of hours' flight direct from my house in Royston, with free parking of course, comes with the flip side of some rather questionable meals, like the chocolate-covered mealworms that Matt Roberts once tucked into (Matt had already worked with me at the BBC for four or five years or so before then, but he's a gullible lad and has probably eaten worse), or a surprise dive-bombing like the one poor old Virgil the truck mechanic was subjected to.

I actually dive-bombed a ferry on another occasion, on the way to the Isle of Man. I knew Bernard Murray was sailing over so I called him and asked what time his crossing was. 'We're halfway across,' he said. So I caught up with the boat and did three fly-bys, as close as I could possibly get to it. I had Bernard on the phone, standing on the deck, and I'm saying, 'Can you see me?' and he's going, 'No!' It turned out I had the wrong ferry! God knows what the poor captain of this one thought was going on.

Flying became a real passion of mine and along with some friends including Barry and his helicopter instructor Pete Barnes, Jeremy Paxton and Julian Seddon – Jeremy and Julian were also helicopter pilots – we formed a tight group that we called 'The Squadron'. Jeremy made the papers once when he was asked to fly Shirley Bassey to Glastonbury, only to be forced into an emergency landing in a field due to fog. Poor old Shirley was so desperate for a piss she had to run off into a little old lady's house and use the bathroom!

Sadly, Julian and I are the only members of The Squadron still alive. Barry was the first to go, followed ten years later by Pete, who was killed in a quite infamous incident when he flew his helicopter into a crane in central London. Just a couple of weeks after that Jeremy had a massive coronary and died in his bed. All three of them were just 53 years old.

Now, as much as ever, I live to make sure that I don't die wondering and put whatever time I have to good use. A couple of winters ago I was chatting to James Whitham, who had been doing a stage tour with Foggy called *Giving It Gas*, and Whit was telling me that whenever they ran out of stories they started using mine! So I spoke to my good friend and agent Mike Rowland, with whom I worked on similar projects like the big stage show at Motorcycle Live, and with some help from Michelle we came up with our own version. Much to my surprise my daughter Frankie loved the idea too so we brought her in and called it the MAD (My Adolescent Dad) Tour. I had no idea Frankie could be as confident or as funny as she is on stage and it has all worked out perfectly. We spend the winter months planning the show and then tour it around the country from February to April, with some extra dates after the racing season finishes in October.

Essentially Frankie is the host and interviewer, posing the kind of questions to her father that any daughter would probably rather not hear the answers to, and I tell my tales of the times when PC stood for Pulling Crumpet. Sadly the Politically Correct brigade have tried to suck the fun out of my life, but even in these hypersensitive modern times I believe the show must go on and the reaction I have had to it suggests many other people share my view.

Performing in theatres has been a wonderful experience. People ask me if I ever get bored of doing the same show every time, but I don't, because it's a different audience every time. They react to it differently. I have done a lot of after dinner speaking over the years and you are never quite sure how you are going down, because half of the people have their backs to you and there's a lot going on in the room. In a theatre, the audience is brought right in to you, you can hear every little snigger, and I can understand why actors adore the theatre. The whole atmosphere is with you and it's quite addictive.

It makes my Januarys a lot better because I'm planning for that. No matter what you do, I think it's important to feel useful. Also, I get to spend time with my beautiful, funny daughter, of whom I am incredibly proud. Working together has been a great opportunity to bond and get to understand each other, and her Father's Day message to me on Facebook last year summed our relationship up. 'Happy Father's Day to My Adolescent Dad. You're a moron but I love ya!' I can't ask for any more than that. My son Joe has a good job in the aviation industry and works all over the world, but even though he is more hardened, like me, we have a great relationship too and I am very proud of his business acumen and work ethic. I just know that the boy will go far.

I am proud of this because for much of their lives, even though I didn't realise it, I was doing everything I could to distance myself from them. After all those years as a racer, my focus was still on myself and my career. I never showed my emotions, I treated my life and my family flippantly and I took everything around me for granted. Once the racing had finished, I replaced the adrenaline rush and the danger of getting away with something you're not supposed to by having affairs.

Ruth got fed up with all of that, and rightly so, but I think the straw that finally broke the camel's back was when we were having this big dinner party at our farmhouse. We got into a row about something or other and she'd baked this big pavlova and I pied her in the face with it in front of all the guests. That pretty much tipped her over the edge. She said I was the 'Parrish with no limits' and she was probably right.

Ruth demanded a divorce and in 2003 she got it. The house got sold and split up between us and it was a big shock to me. None of that had been in my plan and the whole thing threw me completely off kilter. The house was my life's work; a beautiful building with 12 acres of land, outbuildings with my workshops in them, tennis courts and all the rest of it. We had only just finished having it done up when I suddenly found myself kicked out on my arse with nothing of importance to show for myself. Understandably the kids were upset with me too, so they went with Ruth and I scooted off to the Isle of Man in a temper, taking my van with a few bits and bobs in it, and ended up renting a flat there on my own. I found a girlfriend for a while but I went through a long period of loneliness, during which time I came to the conclusion that I had completely fucked up.

It was a difficult learning curve but finally I understood that I had to care more for the people around me otherwise I was going to be lonely for a long time, so I made a plan while I was out there that if I did find somebody else I would treat them with more respect. It was around this time that I sat down with Suzi Perry and apologised for the way I'd been with her and I would like to think that in general I became a much nicer person to be around. My wife and kids still saw me as a complete arsehole for a long time, but I am proud to have turned things around to the point where we all had Christmas dinner together last year – Ruth and her new husband Chris included.

Given that things have turned out so well I can honestly look back now and say I wouldn't change any of it. Living on the edge, racing motorbikes, flying aeroplanes and shagging girls was all part of who I was at the time. Most of that has gone now, either because I have grown up or because I've just got fed up with being in trouble, but I suppose you could say I'm a prehistoric adrenaline junkie who survived!

In truth I feel lucky that so many circumstances turned into positive opportunities. If my bike had started at Silverstone in 1984, would I have ever become a television commentator? If Mark Phillips hadn't crashed at Donington Park, would I be working now as an expert witness? And Barry. If it wasn't for Barry, I would surely never even have made it as a bike racer, never mind a Truck Racing World Champion. And I certainly would never have enjoyed such a lunatic life.

Good fortune has played a huge part and I don't need anybody to point that out to me. I lost at least nineteen good friends through racing, with two more suffering severe brain damage, and I know that almost any one of them could have been me. As Barry always said, if I fell into a cesspit I'd come up with a salmon on my head and he was right; the fact that I am here to tell these stories has nothing to do with skill or bravery, just luck. And I have had more of that than most.

Epilogue

Well, it might be the end of the book but it's the start of a new chapter for me. It sounds ridiculous but with the combined age of 118, Michelle and I ran off to Yorkshire to secretly get married. We didn't even tell our children we were getting married, as we wanted it to be a quiet affair, and in the beautiful surroundings of Crathorne Hall the deed was done! Everything in my life has revolved around cars, trucks and bikes so it's a bit like I've been leasing her for the past fourteen years and I had the choice to hand her back, or pay the balloon payment, which I've done. So I kind of own her now and I'm fairly confident that she'll appreciate it over the coming years . . . . Poor, poor Michelle!

I'll say that again, Steve! Poor me, arriving in the President's Suite for the wedding ceremony armed with weighing scales and a life-sized cardboard cut-out of Dean Martin. Steve certainly made me and the registrars gasp. You can imagine nothing is straightforward with Steve: the ceremony, the vows or the music . . . producing scales for me to stand on during the ceremony and the vows.

His to me:

My mate
For better and not much worser
For richer and not much poorer
To love and to cherish
From this day forward and not to increase in weight by more
than 2kg – (64kg at the moment?)
I will expect to be on equal terms as Teddy and Holby City
I will give you my heart and all the sex that is required and
should be reciprocal but only to me
Finally you must at times own up to being wrong and then I
will brake earlier
I promise to maintain and cherish you for as long as I can as I
really love you with all my heart
Now with this ring I will now own you.

After composing myself, and waiting for the giggles from the registrars to stop, stepping off the scales it was my turn.

Mine to him:

You are my lover, my best friend
I am your accomplice and stooge, the brunt of your jokes,
You make me laugh, scream and cry but
I will love you, hold you and honour you,
I will respect you, encourage you and cherish you,
In health and sickness,
Through sorrow and success,
For all the days of my life remembering we won't die
wondering.

More laughter and applause. We were now married and walked out of the room to Steve's choice of music, 'The Ying Tong Song', causing more sniggers.

Feeling quite blessed as the snow had fallen, Steve had arranged for an old Norton motorcycle to be waiting outside for our photographs, so all in all the perfect end to a perfect day on becoming Mrs Steve Parrish!

And now we are married I thought we should sit down and talk about Steve's immaturity. His reply was, fine, but not whilst the conkers season is on. You're only young once but you can be immature all your life!